REQUIEM FOR THE LIVING

JEFF METCALF

REQUIEM FOR THE LIVING

A Memoir

THE UNIVERSITY OF UTAH PRESS | SALT LAKE CITY

PUBLISHED IN COOPERATION WITH THE UTAH DIVISION
OF ARTS AND MUSEUMS

Winner of the 2012 Original Writing Competition for Creative Nonfiction.
Published in cooperation with the Utah Division of Arts and Museums.

 The Defiance House Man colophon is a registered trademark of the
University of Utah Press. It is based on a four-foot-tall Ancient
Puebloan pictograph (late PIII) near Glen Canyon, Utah.

18 17 16 15 14   1 2 3 4 5

Library of Congress Cataloging-in-Publication Data
Library of Congress Control Number: 2014948365
CIP data on file with the Library of Congress

Printed and bound by Sheridan Books, Inc., Ann Arbor, Michigan.

for
Alana, Bailey, John, Jack, Finn, and Dave

my siblings,
Sue and Barry

and my parents,
Jack and Mary

Contents

Baptism

Promise

Drifting

Contents

Being

BAPTISM

The Killing Fields

I'm hell-bent on writing an essay a week for a year.

It's a straightforward enough plan and I need this sort of discipline right now. I'm dealing with an aggressive form of prostate cancer and the drugs I've been administered over the past nine years have lost their potency. They have done a good job of keeping the cancer cells at bay but the rodeo is over.

In the course of the nine years since my diagnosis, I've been cut open, had my prostate removed, discovered that the cancer cells had spilled outside the margins, spent eight weeks in radiation, and, when that procedure wasn't successful, I began a series of Lupron injections backed up with a Casodex kicker and Zytiga. Lupron floods my body with female hormones which suppress the development of testosterone, a necessary component for the cancer cells to survive. My side effects have included hot flashes, loss of muscle tone, decreased libido, depression, loss of body hair, mood swings, frequent insomnia, and the retention of water.

Essentially, my body has no idea what it is or how to act and it's confusing. It's also funny, and humor counts against cancer, trust me.

My blood draws have become increasingly more frequent because my PSA continues to rise. The climate has changed. There is less small chat, something I have always enjoyed on my frequent visits to the hospital. I've known these nurses and doctors for several years now. What they don't want to say is this: "You have more time behind you than you do in front of you." I know this and I understand it very well. I also know what comes next. There are a few medical choices for me but none of them are pleasant.

I feel the way I did as a small child when summer vacation was drawing to a close. We all tried to hang on . . . to slow time down, to stretch the limits of summer against the simple fact that school would start and there was nothing we could do to stay the tide. I'm trying to do the same with cancer given the science standing in front of me, but it's not enough. Summer ends. School begins.

My drugs, the ones I have loathed because of what they have done to me, have served their purpose. What looms ahead of me now is more complicated. What I have learned over these several years is that, at least in this country, the patient is not necessarily the first consideration in the protocol for any treatment. I'm fortunate, because I have good insurance. To a great degree, I am alive because of this insurance and the skill of the doctors attached to the hospitals I have frequented. What happens to those less fortunate? It is a rhetorical question. We already know the answer. They die.

Still, when it comes to the practice of medicine I have some deep underlying concerns about the relationship between the equation of hospitals, drug companies, and insurance companies. There are drugs currently on the market in various stages of clinical trials that might be of help in slowing down the advance of this cancer. The caveat, however, is that the most promising can only be administered when the cancer has metastasized to the bones. From a patient's point of view, this makes little sense. "In other words, you are telling me that the drug could be effective but it can only be approved by the insurance company and hospital protocol after it is deep in my bones." This sort of convoluted pretzel logic needs to be called into question and the patient needs to be extremely proactive and vocal about such reasoning. It is not rational by any means.

A former doctor of mine once accused me of being "disagreeable" because I seemed to frequently "challenge" protocols that he discussed with me. These protocols seemed to revere the position of the pharmaceutical and insurance companies over the patient. He reminded me, in no uncertain terms, that it was he who, in fact, practiced medicine, and not I. I, in turn, and with perhaps a bit less guarded enthusiasm, reminded him that it was "I" who practiced "living" and, in no uncertain terms, wanted to do so for as long as I possibly could. Shortly after this "spat," we divorced each other.

It was only recently in a visit to my oncologist and with specific regard to the above-mentioned, "wait until the cancer metastasizes to the bones" explanation, that I dropped the mother of all challenges and invoked the *Oath of Hippocrates*. I simply observed that Hippocrates would find great disappointment in prevailing medical practices that placed institutions and other agencies above the patient's well-being.

My comment was meant to provoke discourse and it most certainly did. But, it also invited examination and inclusion. I have, along with my doctor's clinical researcher, a gifted and talented woman, begun to talk of possibilities "outside of the box." I have morphed from a statistic to a face, and an integral part of this equation. I can live with this.

In all fairness, I've become acquainted with many of the nurses, interns, technologists, and doctors who have attended to me during this journey. With some, I have become friends, out beyond the world of medicine. They are interesting people, great company, and dedicated fully to their profession. When I go to see the magicians, I can oftentimes discern much by the language of a face. If the news is less than promising, there is an economy of words. In short, it's safe to say that, indeed, I have more time behind me than in front of me. But, in the end, can't we all say this? Who truly knows, really?

A few summers ago, I spent a weekend retreat with men who have and are recovering from cancer. A "specialist" trained in dealing with men in various stages of the disease guided the discussion group. One question asked of us all was, "What has cancer contributed to your life . . . good or bad?" Several men replied by saying they were thankful because cancer had taught them to live more and to spend more time with their families. "I've taken more time to smell the roses since I've had cancer," an older gentleman offered. I felt sorry for him.

Michael Ortiz Hill and Deena Metzger, coauthors of a chapbook from Elik Press called *Sacred Illness, Sacred Medicine*, speak to disease as a teacher and a guide. Metzger offers us this insight: "'Cancer has designed a path that has been life-giving to me and others. I could not have designed such a program myself; spirit had to intervene." She later comments that "if we are conscious, it can call us, and the society around us, into a different life." It is an interesting thought.

Cancer, or any other debilitating or terminal disease, can offer us personal insight; and on an academic level, I completely understand how these people have compartmentalized their disease.

But I'm very simple when it comes to the cancer in my body. I don't want to own it . . . to walk down the sidewalk letting it instruct me. I want to stomp it into the ground, eradicate it from my body. It is not welcome.

The work I do at the university and deep in my community working for social justice is powerful medicine for me. I have always been alive and fully engaged in everything I do. This is a gift. Cancer sucks. Cancer is a great inconvenience for people who like to live.

I'm going to claw for every minute I have left in this world.

If anything, cancer has made me think about cleaning the garage. I have kept journals, handwritten journals, for many years. I actually don't remember when I began keeping them. They are filled with short-story ideas, partially rendered plays, recipes, notes on great afternoons of fly-fishing, close inspection of teaching and politics, and observations about myself and my family—and always about food.

I expected to retire and spend time writing, organizing sections of these journals into a tightly crafted narrative. A book about living in Holland post–World War II or a book about having the opportunity to live in the Middle East for five years and traveling freely through the open markets of Al Kobar and playing with Bedouin children. It has been a splendid, extremely rich life. No regrets except . . . except I'd like to get some of this down in an organized fashion. I am guilty of putting my writing on the backburner for far too long. It is time to pay the piper.

The Door

The front door to 131 Silver Lake Road opened outward, not to a view of manicured lawns carefully bordered by rows of brilliantly colored flowers, but to the dark, dank underbelly of a tenement building that my grandfather managed. It was a door without warmth, no mullioned glass windows or brass-plated nametags with family crests. Instead, it was a door of riveted sheet metal, painted and chipped, dented and beaten like my family's early days.

We lived underground, below the street, in a world without light, without shape, without energy. Our only windows were distorted glass panes, set high above the kitchen table, which looked out onto the sidewalk at street level. Instead of seeing children playing stickball or hop scotch, or watching couples stroll by, headed to the front stoop of the tenement to drink cold Ballantine beer and listen to the radio, we saw ankles. Until I was six years old I could only recognize people by the shape and carry of their feet. Nurse Crawley, her gait light and airy, her feet almost lifting off into flight. Pat Zapalack, my father's drinking buddy, solid strides, a man rooted to the ground, his thick leather Redwing work boots well oiled and cared for. Mrs. Quebler's swollen feet, skin pinched and forced into a pair of navy blue, open-toed high heels, her toes squeezed together like fat little sausages. And then there were Jake Fisher's beefy, broad-footed, black butcher's shoes caked in blood and sawdust. Jake the Slum Lord. Jake the Collector. Jake the Butcher. When we children saw those shoes waddling in a rounded half step, we knew it was time to turn off the radio, shut off the lights, remain absolutely silent, and not answer the door.

"It's sort of like hide-and-seek," my mother would whisper, but we all knew better.

Gypsy Life

When I was not quite two years old, my family moved from San Francisco to New York, where my father accepted a job working for Standard Oil. While my parents squirreled away money for a down payment on a home, we pressed ourselves into the cramped, subterranean space of my mother's parents, Rosy and Walter.

Walter was "Pops" to us and he was an important man. His job as the superintendent of our building—a twenty-five-unit complex on Silver Lake Road in Staten Island—was, in my estimation, the most important job in the world. Following dinner, which we ate outside the apartment in the damp hallway because the living space was too small, I would often help Pops haul garbage from the dumbwaiters to the garbage cans stored in the old coal room.

On the belt of his dungarees, Pops wore a large key chain that was attached to a retractable cord and he knew the key to every storage unit and mechanical room by touch. Clearly, he was a magician.

My older sister, Susan, and I slept on a Murphy hide-a-bed in the living room that was separated from the kitchen by a brightly colored muslin sheet. Our younger brother, Barry, slept in my parents' room in a cardboard box decorated with pictures from Life and National Geographic magazines.

My father's job in Manhattan required that he take a bus to the Staten Island Ferry Terminal, a thirty-minute ride to the city, then two subway connects and a good brisk walk to his office. Every morning he would join Rosy in the kitchen for coffee and Lucky Strike cigarettes before disappearing into darkness. Rosy, a devout Catholic, would attend early morning mass before leaving for her job as a switchboard operator.

Years later, when I was forced to attend catechism, I wondered what possible egregious sins my grandmother could have committed to require such atonement.

I would often awaken to the aroma of stiff coffee and fried bacon mixed with the pungent smell of cigarettes wafting through the apartment. It was the laughter, though, that would draw me from the comfort of warm covers into the kitchen where I was always welcome to join in this ritual.

My special drink was a hot cup of Bosco that Rosy would ladle into a ceramic coffee mug just like hers. She would often place a fresh Kaiser roll, smothered with butter and layered with bacon, in front of me. I would blow on my Bosco and devour the roll while quietly listening to them speak in a chorus of mysterious adult gibberish that made absolutely no sense to me. What counted most was the fact that I was welcome and that I was included in this cramped space.

One humid summer evening my parents returned to the apartment with four cardboard boxes of pizza from Happy Days Pizzeria and a case of cold Knickerbocker beer. They had an announcement to make. We set up cardboard tables outside in the courtyard and prepared for a celebration. I was allowed, under the watchful eyes of Pops, to use an ice pick to fill a washtub with chipped shards of ice and pack it with beer and sodas. Rosy lit punks to fend off mosquitoes and, once lit, pushed them into small containers filled with sand. My sister and I could only imagine the cause of this celebration.

My father began with a toast, thanking Rosy and Walter for their graciousness and generosity in allowing us to live with them while they looked for a house. And then, in a stunning revelation, my mother announced that they had, in fact, successfully purchased a home on Raleigh Avenue, not far from the Staten Island Zoo. Judging by the reaction of both grandparents and my own parents, this seemed to be wonderful news. What I understood of the moment was that we would no longer be living with my grandparents and, more disturbing to me, that we would be leaving the Silver Lake neighborhood that I loved for its rich mix of all different kinds of people and move across town to the other side of the world. This did not sit well with me. I looked at my sister's face to check her reaction. She was smiling and this concerned me deeply. Even at this early age, we were sworn enemies. If she was happy it only confirmed the fact that I should be wary of the events to follow.

I remember asking her if this was a good thing and she gave me "the look" which would always suggest that I was born to my station in life as a second-class citizen in the workings of the world.

"We'll probably get our own room so I won't have to sleep next to you," she said.

This came as rather a shock to me, the idea of my own room. But the greater insult was that my sister was offended by having to share the Murphy hide-a-bed with me. Clearly, I was the one who had suffered the greater pains of this injustice. The moment was getting more and more confusing.

We would move from the Silver Lake apartments within a week and the following week we were in our new home. Although I had a bedroom of my own and an actual yard with trees, I was not happy. To register the severity of my disappointment in a way that I was certain my parents would understand, I announced I was running away from home and was never coming back. My sister reacted with exuberance and my mother, thoughtful as she would always be, helped me pack some things in a bandana before I hit the open road.

I spent the day putzing about in the adjacent woods in a series of explorations that included filling my pockets with pea pods to fit my pea-shooter and crafting a couple of spears out of sticks in case I had to fight off wild animals. I constructed forts out of branches and tried to build the internal framework for a teepee but failed miserably. There were things I needed from the house to craft this new Utopia, but a return to our home now would signal failure.

By early evening I was getting hungry. Still, a stubborn streak prevented me from surrender. When it began to get dark, I moved closer to our home. I was distracted for some time with chasing fireflies and then, suddenly, the woods began to erupt into a chorus of night sounds unfamiliar to me. There were sounds that were bigger than my imagination could handle. These were not the sounds of my former neighborhood but sounds foreign to me. Dangerous sounds. Things darted through the air in swift and erratic patterns. Bats. I looked to the kitchen window where I could see my family having dinner, illuminated in an inviting glow of light. I began to cry.

When my mother opened the door she welcomed me back with terrific fanfare. My sister actually slid over and made a space for me alongside her on the kitchen bench. My father filled a cereal bowl with buttery macaroni and cheese and asked me to recount my adventures.

At first, I was reluctant. Certainly, I deserved some sort of punishment and this smelled like a trap, but I quickly acquiesced and wove a story of daring adventure and exploration that, I was certain, rivaled the experiences of Lewis and Clark. I was not interrupted in this moment; not by my sister who would have been more than happy to offer the Latin names of all the species of plants and insects I had described; nor by my younger brother who had recently taken to chewing glass and could be of some distraction at the dinner table; and certainly not by my parents who, I was convinced, were completely and utterly engaged by my narrative. The beauty of that moment was that my family listened to me with great attention and interest.

For the next two weeks, my mother and father cleaned and painted the interior of the house, hung Flash Gordon wallpaper in my bedroom, ballerina wallpaper in my sister's, and characters from Disney World in my brother's bedroom.

At night, with the door to my bedroom left slightly ajar, light seeped along the back wall and I imagined myself exploring other galaxies. It was such a pleasant way to fall asleep. It was almost impossible to imagine such wealth and good fortune could have befallen us.

I adapted quickly to these new surroundings and became acutely aware that my status at John Tyler School, P.S. 45 on St. Lawrence Avenue, a run-down elementary school that smelled of Lysol and Clorox, was clearly on the rise.

One month after moving into our home on Raleigh Avenue, my father returned home from work with an earth-shaking announcement that would forever change the shape of how I would see the world. He had been offered a promotion of some significance but it would require that we move from Staten Island to Den Hague, Holland.

We sat at the dinner table as he explained the particulars. He was excited and animated as he began to detail the proposition to us. I shifted uneasily in my seat and studied my sister's face carefully for any signs of alarm. I could detect none. He'd been given twenty-four hours to decide, and then the offer was off the table.

My parents weighed the pros and cons of such a move. Although I was quite certain my father was excited about the offer, I couldn't get a read from my mother. Finally, and without hesitation, my mother said, "Let's flip a coin. Heads we leave for a new adventure and tails, we stay." My father pulled a quarter from his pocket and flipped it into the air. I would like to say that I remembered it slowly turning in the air, but in truth, I was stunned when it landed on the kitchen table heads up. "So be it," my mother said, and suggested in the same breath that my father call his boss immediately to let him know we'd be thrilled. Thrilled was not the word that came to my mind.

Three weeks after the flip of a coin, we arrived in Holland and were driven by limousine to the Kasteel de Wittenberg Hotel where we would live for a month before moving onto Ambassador Row in Den Hague. Shortly after we had adjusted to our new home, my sister and I would enter the International School of the Hague and I would be placed in Mrs. Kent's second-grade class in a lower primary school. None of us, including our parents, had the faintest idea how our world would change. But my mother believed, in both practice and in spirit, that one should never pass up an adventure and life was not worth living unless it was lived to the fullest. For her, and certainly later on for her children, it was not an empty cliché, it was practiced.

Giving Up the Ghost

Religion is like asking people if they like lamb or cilantro. If it doesn't work, it doesn't work. You can't convert the unconvertible.

I was born into Catholicism. Not much choice, really. Because my parents were Catholic we kids assumed the mantle. For some time it worked, based primarily on fear and nothing else. I received my first communion when my family lived in Amsterdam, Holland, in 1956. I was seven years old.

My parents would drive the three children to catechism in a small Catholic church where we would meet other ex-pats, kids our same age who were also living in the Netherlands. I liked meeting other kids who shared the same language. I learned mass in Latin and became an altar boy. I worked the bells and liked the pageantry. If I did funerals, I could actually make some money. When I was short on money, I would pray that somebody in the parish would die.

Money was a good thing and I thought about becoming a priest until I discovered priests had to be celibate and they took a vow of poverty. At the time, I didn't exactly know what being celibate meant but judging from the older boys' conversations, I learned it had something to do with not using one's penis and I had become quite fond of mine.

My favorite part of the mass was the sacramental wine. Wine that would become the blood of Christ. Just a bit creepy, but when we snuck some, it tasted great. It made me warm and mass would just sort of blow by.

I didn't do well in the confessional booth, a sacred space where Catholics confessed their most serious sins. It works like this: The priest hears confession on certain days. Sinners line up outside a confessional booth to confess their sins. The confessional is like a small closet, divided down the middle so there is a compartment on each side. In the wall is an open passageway, perhaps the size of a small window, with a lattice or curtain that, in theory, obscures the penitent from the priest. The priest sits on one side and the sinner kneels on a kneeler on the other and begins the Sacrament of Penance.

There is, of course, ritual and the penitent offers the following declaration: "Bless me Father for I have sinned. It has been 'x' weeks since my last confession and during that time I have committed the following sins." At this point, a sinner, say like myself, would list the sins and the priest would grant forgiveness and admonish the penitent to offer a series of "Our Father" or "Hail Mary" prayers to complete the Act of Forgiveness. The final two steps in the procedure were critical. The sinner then performed a prayer to the priest called the Act of Contrition. And finally, after leaving the confessional, the penitent would kneel at a pew bench inside the body of the church and perform the required prayers.

In the confessional, I worked on my own "layaway" plan of sins. I would often heap up a pile of made-up sins as insurance, a down payment of sorts on my next batch of sins. It seemed like a smart plan to stay ahead of the game. Once, I confessed that I had committed adultery and coveted my neighbor's wife. It so startled the priest that he slid open the panel, looked at me, and said, "Young man, do you have any idea what adultery means?"

"No, Father."

"Then don't confess to something you didn't do! It's a sin."

"Yes, Father."

This sinning stuff was complicated.

When I was eleven and a half, my family moved from Holland to Saudi Arabia. At the time, practicing any religion other than Islam was forbidden. Thursday and Friday were the weekends of the Islamic calendar and Saturday and Sunday just another part of the work week. Foreigners were obliged to follow the same calendar. Mass was celebrated on Friday at the local movie theater. I attended catechism, which was held clandestinely in our teacher's home in preparation for my Sacrament of Confirmation.

Our catechism teacher, Mr. Steensma, was a former Jesuit priest who taught math and coached basketball at the school. He was a "cool" and "hip" teacher and all the girls had crushes on him. Mr. Steensma encouraged us to openly discuss and examine our religion. No question or observation about the practice of religion would be considered out of bounds. In theory, it was a fabulous idea. In practice, however, it began to deconstruct almost immediately. Whenever anybody got too close, asked questions that were complicated, Steensma would verbally punish . . . no, humiliate . . . no, embarrass them. Soon the catechism class was all but silenced. Steensma quizzed us like a drill sergeant and we replied to his grilling in rote response.

Once, in class, I suggested that confession seemed like an unnecessary ritual, and quite frankly, a burden on God. It seemed to me, I'd argued, that God was too busy with really important matters to be interrupted by such trivial distractions. A sinner sinned. If he/she truly regretted the act and seemed penitent, it should be enough. In other words—and I can now see this as a great error in my judgment of Steensma's open-and-frank policy of "anything goes"—I said, "So why doesn't the Pope create an edict that just cuts out the middleman?" This might have been the final straw for Steensma. He completely came unhinged and went after me. In fairness to Steensma, I'd been pushing his buttons.

On the day of Confirmation, we were all properly scrubbed and dressed in our finery. We sat together at the front of the theater waiting to be called to the stage. On the given nod by one of our catechism teachers, we would walk onto the stage behind the curtain and wait until our name was called.

We knew our catechism and understood the significance of the perfection of Baptism in the rite of this sacred ceremony. We'd carefully selected our patron saint, who would become our protector and intercessor in heaven. All we had to do was walk across the stage, genuflect in front of the bishop, kiss the pinky ring, make our promise to God, be anointed with chrism (a consecrated oil), and receive the bishop's words, "Be sealed with the Gift of the Holy Spirit."

Waiting in line for my turn, I had my first and only religious epiphany. It was simple. I realized, given all that I had witnessed and understood about my own religion and carrying these observations into the larger world to encompass all major religions, that I didn't believe any of it.

From my vantage point, I could see my family sitting proudly in the front of the theater. When my name was called, I walked across the stage, nodded at the bishop, and exited out the back door of the theater. There was an audible gasp from the audience. The last thing I remember hearing was the heavy theater door latching behind me and forever locking me out of that world.

The Battle of Hastings

Ms. Stiles was tough. She was old, too. Really old . . . maybe in her mid-twenties. She was British, as were most of the teachers at the International School of the Hague in Holland, which adhered to the strict Calvin system. She had red hair in a Prince Valiant cut and she smelled of Gouda cheese. At least, this is the way I remember her.

My first day in class, I was so nervous my feet were moving up and down like a sewing machine. Ms. Stiles walked up and down each row with a yardstick that she would wield like a broadaxe. She stopped alongside my desk and told me if I didn't stop my infernal dancing she would chop my feet off with a paper cutter. I had no doubt at the time that she meant it. She was that scary and that convincing.

In Ms. Stiles's class, the goof-ups sat at the back of the room and that was fine by me. There was more space for my feet. Keeping me company on the back row was Nigel H., this droopy-eyed English kid who just didn't seem to get anything right in class, and Danny K., who had the largest ears of any human being I had ever met or would meet in my life.

Nigel once told me he had been dropped on his head a number of times when he was born and that was why he was so dumb. I had little reason to doubt him because he had a funny-looking narrow head, sort of like . . . well, he'd been dropped on his head several times. I never thought he was dumb. Ms. Stiles would often ask him if he was an idiot, which she pronounced, "Idjit" in her highbrow toffee English accent. It never seemed to bother Nigel. He'd simply say, "Yes, Mrs. Stiles. Probably." But what Ms. Stiles never understood was that Nigel was a storehouse of really cool information, it just didn't happen to be the stuff Ms. Stiles asked him about. Wars, historic battles, torture methods of the Medievals. That was his specialty.

Nigel didn't shuffle his feet like I did, but he kind of mumbled to himself, did battle, I guess. That's what it sounded like. Every so often you'd hear the *sswooosh* (an arrow from a crossbow) followed by a *thwump* (piercing through the chain-mail armor of some enemy, probably Ms. Stiles) trailed by the *aaahhh* (of that same villain falling off the castle wall into the ocean far below). He was fantastic, drawing out the fall until it ended in a very faint splash. His artwork always dealt with knights and wars. He drew the most detailed castles, with moats and drawbridges; great battle scenes with dead bodies, and decapitated soldiers, and fallen horses with arrows stuck out of them, and archers with crossbows and longbows and catapults launching fiery cannonballs, and a guy with incredibly long arms pouring boiling oil over the castle wall on to unsuspecting enemy soldiers who were using battering rams at the front gate. He was a great artist by third-grade standards.

Once, on a dumb day, Ms. Stiles asked the class what famous battle took place in 1066. The class, to a person, even Monica G., who knew everything, sat there, dumb. Ms. Stiles was boiling. We were losers. Suddenly, Nigel's hand shot up in the air. I was incredulous. I looked at him like, "Not today, Nigel." I thought, "This would not be the day to piss Ms. Stiles off." The rub was, there was nobody else in class Ms. Stiles could call on. Nigel was the only one in class with his hand up. And he was confident.

Ms. Stiles asked the question again. There was a pleading look in her eyes. But Nigel's hand was slashing back and forth like a windshield wiper. She had absolutely no other choice but to acknowledge Nigel. To this day, I think she actually went into a stall, that moment in teaching where she had no way out but to call on the "Idjit." My feet were moving up and down with such vigor my desk was moving out of the back row, and Danny K. was pulling on his ears so hard that I thought his eyes might roll back in his head like a slot machine.

Finally and reluctantly, Ms. Stiles acknowledged Nigel. "Nigel," Ms. Stiles said, her voice offering a forewarning of sorts, "do you think you know the answer? Do you really think you know what important battle took place on . . ."

"Yes!" Nigel blasted out, before Ms. Stiles could finish her sentence. "The Battle of Hastings! 1066! William of Normandy crossed the English Channel to fight the Saxon King Harold II. The battle began on October 14th in the early morning and William of Normandy was triumphant and claimed the English crown to become the King of England. He became known as William the Conqueror! Harold II was killed on the battlefield, shot in the eye with an arrow."

Nigel went on for a full five minutes describing the feigned retreats and how when Harold's army chased after the Norman troops, William's boys hacked them up pretty good. He went on and on detailing every significant battle strategy with absolute passion and clarity.

Ms. Stiles just stood there in front of the class, slack-jawed and dumbfounded. Nigel the Idjit, Nigel Who Often Wore His Sister's Angora Sweater, Nigel of the Perfect Hair, Nigel Lord of the Back Row, was a freakin' medieval scholar.

The class was enraptured by Nigel's passion. Ms. Stiles finally had to stop Nigel from his lecture or he would have continued on through recess, which would have been fine by all of us. He was a fabulous teacher. It was a stellar moment in third grade history. From that day on, we all saw Nigel in a different light. Nigel H., in his unassuming way, in his shy and accepting way, held his own secret mysteries. He was not the "Idjit" Ms. Stiles thought he was. He was a quiet young boy full of curiosity and a hunger for knowledge. Nigel H. was a teacher and we, a ragtag group of third graders, were his students. On that day, we all owed Nigel for having bailed our collective third-grade cans out of the fire.

The Battle of Hastings is in me still. It resides deep in grey matter and I had no idea, then, how much this moment would inform me later in my life as a teacher.

Indirectly, Ms. Stiles had given us a great lesson in teaching by attempting to humiliate one of our own. What I think I came to understand, although I could never have articulated it at the moment, was this: we are all teachers and we are all students and this journey is always in constant motion.

I am indeed in Nigel's debt.

Hung

I'll admit that part of the incident might have been my fault. But, in my own defense, I was a fourth grader in Ms. DeHarris's class at the International School in the Netherlands and there was very little I could do "right" as far as she was concerned.

My older sister, the genius, had been one of her students and I was, by all measure, a terrific disappointment. Part of my job, when we formed a pen pal correspondence with a sister school in the United Kingdom, was to write the class letter. It was the only thing in the fourth grade I did well. When I wasn't weaving these fantastic tales of adventure and danger, I worked almost full-time at being the class clown.

Ms. DeHarris would not have delegated that responsibility to me of her own accord, but Principal Whitehead had insisted that I be the "Official Scribe." And that was that. There was nothing, absolutely nothing, at Ms. DeHarris's disposal that could work against me. And, for a fourth-grade student, such elevated status was indeed a wonderful and joyous event. I would like to say I penned some of the finest prose the fourth grade had ever witnessed. Classics, such as *Tarzan and Dart Fight the Monster Gorilla* and *Danger at the Brussels World Fair* were daring literature in the day. I took my profession seriously. To not do so would have been churlish.

On the last day of school, Ms. DeHarris would bring treats to class and just before we were dismissed for the summer, she would call each student to the front of the room and bestow upon them a prediction of the future. I could not wait. Because my position of power and privilege as the Official Scribe had granted me such schoolyard respect, I had no idea what baptism Ms. DeHarris would offer. It had to be good. For all her nastiness, I must admit that Ms. DeHarris was truly one of the first feminists I'd ever met.

The predictions were done in alphabetical order. Margaret was going to be the first female Member of Parliament and Nigel would become a Medieval Scholar at Cambridge. This was better than anyone could have hoped for under any circumstance. I worried about my classmate Danny Keely, who was, before my elevated status as a writer, my comedic equal. In truth, however, he was much better than I. His impersonation of Alfred Hitchcock doing Adolph Hitler was sheer genius, placing him in a league of his own. When Ms. DeHarris predicted he would be the next Jerry Lewis, the class went wild.

There was only one student before my prediction and I was getting lightheaded. At the minimum, I would be compared to Franklin Dixon, author of the wildly popular Hardy Boys detective thrillers. My secret desire, and I realized this would extend beyond Ms. DeHarris's generosity and imagination, would be to be compared to Edgar Rice Burroughs. It would be the capstone of my writing career.

My name was called and I flew to the front of the classroom. The crowd was on my side. I looked at Ms. DeHarris and she smiled at me. For the first time I could ever remember, she looked beautiful. And today, again for the first time as far back as I could remember, she didn't look angry.

"Jeff," she began, "You will be the first person from this class to be hung from the gallows."

Clearly, I had misunderstood. I looked out at the class. Their faces were frozen, stunned. It could not be. Not after my epic penning of *Bird Boy of the Tundra*. She must have made a serious mistake.

"Right, now," she said, patting my arm and sticking a sucker in my hand. "Back to your seat. We've others to do, don't we?"

I sat at my desk fighting back tears. Buppee Tarqueeny patted me on the shoulder. Danny Keely tried to get me to laugh with his Alfred Hitchcock impersonation. None of it worked. I could only think about one thing. What would it feel like when the gallows dropped?

Hongerwinter

In 1954 my family moved from the basement of my grandparents' tenement apartment in New York to the luxurious and privileged residential area of Wassenar, Holland. The home we moved to was a splendid Dutch brick cottage with a thatched roof. It sat center on three-quarters of an acre of beautiful gardens, a backyard where, most certainly during the war, a garden had been kept and remnants of volunteer plants held firm to the soil.

One afternoon while digging foxholes for an elaborate game of war, I uncovered two small tins of c-rations that had been wrapped in a small piece of canvas. The tins were stamped in bold letters: USAF. Living in Holland, these rations defied any sort of logic. What was the story behind these treasures? If anyone knew, it would be my older sister by eleven months, Sue. She was a genius, the sort of sister that truly did know "everything," something I could not have possibly admitted to her then.

Under Susan's direction, and with the help of a half-dozen kids from the neighborhood, we systematically began a serious excavation of the site. Influenced by *National Geographic* photographs of archeological digs in Egypt, my sister convinced us to quadrant off areas of the dig site with string. This way, as she explained to all of us, we would have "the story" of these "food-burying" Dutch. It wasn't until later on that same evening we would begin to understand the full impact of what all this meant in a very personal way.

It seemed to me that our parents were less enthusiastic about the discovery than we were. A great deal of this might have been because this became a very serious and sustained dig. At any given time, my mother would find kids wandering through the house, muddy feet, looking for the bathroom or something to eat. My father, who had always been very silent about his activity in World War II, explained to us that toward the end of the war, American and Allied Forces flew peace missions over a large section of the European Theatre dropping food and supplies to a starving civilian population. It sounded, from the point of view of a third grader, like a very decent thing to do.

Frequently my parents were required to spend evenings engaged in socializing for my father's company. This was the golden age of the cocktail party and these soirees were elaborate. It was a decidedly international crowd of men and women who would become the "movers and shakers" of a post–World War II Europe.

When my parents hosted one of these gala events at our home, the house was transformed into something magical. Gardeners would trim, clip, and prune the bushes, while a host of decorators would turn the inside of our home into a nightclub. Throughout the day, deliveries from bakery wagons, vegetable vendors, cheese and meat purveyors, and the alcohol delivery man would pull up and unload food and drink into our kitchen. Our favorite arrival would be that of the ice-wagon where two muscular Dutchmen would unload blocks of ice, filling tubs with Heineken beer, champagne, wine, and chip ice until the bottles would perspire in beads of cold liquid pearls.

It was exciting as the guests began to arrive in entourages of Mercedes, Peugeots, and Citroens. We children would be dressed up in our best clothes waiting at the door to greet the arrivals. When the majority of guests had arrived, we would disappear upstairs where our favorite tender, Mrs. Bopya, would spend time playing and reading to us before we turned in for the night.

Mrs. Bopya was simply the best in the game. Her English and French were absolutely flawless and when she told us bedtime stories, we held onto every word as though our lives depended on it. In reality, we really knew very little about her except for the fact that she had a son and that her husband had died in World War II. Beyond that, she offered very little information about her personal life.

On this evening, we had our own story to share with Mrs. Bopya. As my sister began to reveal the particulars about our ongoing excavation in the backyard, Mrs. Bopya's countenance changed. Instead of the usual attentive and astonished responses she'd previously accorded our stories, Mrs. Bopya became pensive and quiet.

My brother, Barry, asked if she'd like to see our loot and when she agreed, we padded down the stairs, cut through the kitchen, switched on the backyard floodlights and revealed the booty. Under the glare of light, the tins of food, stacked according to the contents—main meals, supplementary sides, and desserts—were pretty impressive.

Mrs. Bopya surveyed the dig, bending down once to pick up a tin of biscuits and then placing it back down neatly on a stack of other tins. As she did so, she mumbled something in Dutch. I took her by the hand. "Come over here," I begged. "This is really cool." Our prize possession of the dig was a short-wave radio. It had been in a wooden box wrapped in heavy canvas. In the several years since the end of the war, the box had begun to rot but the radio appeared to be intact. My father would not allow us to plug it into a socket for fear it might electrocute us. Mrs. Bopya said very little. She was someplace else.

"At the end of the war," she explained, "even though the war was over, the Germans tried to starve us to death. The winter was very cold and there was no food. Our docks were destroyed and the country was flooded. These things happen in war."

"But," my sister interrupted, "the family that lived here kept the food away from the Germans."

"And they kept it away from their neighbors," said Mrs. Bopya. "Many Dutch people starved to death during that winter."

My sister began to ask a question but stopped.

"These were not good people," Mrs. Bopya replied. "They did not share their food with others who needed it."

Mrs. Bopya took us into the house and put us to bed. Before drifting off to sleep, I could hear laughter from the downstairs bar and the music of Louis Armstrong drifting above the din of partygoers. What I could not reconcile was Mrs. Bopya's story in counterpoint to the lavish party just a floor below us. But the story, as only such a story of truth and pain can be carried and offered, was now inside of me, as dark and mysterious as any I would ever carry in my life.

Zola, Queen of the Lilliputians

This is my mother's favorite story. It's a simple one. It's a story about a foreign country, romance, a circus, a midget ringmaster named Zola, and me. Part of the story belongs to my mother's memory and part of the story belongs to me. Somewhere between these two memories is the truth. Sometimes, true stories are about the light.

My mother's last days were spent trying to hold onto the light. Words failed her and the lists of things she was incapable of doing got longer and more onerous. Names of her old friends sat like strange fruits on the end of her tongue. The taste was bitter and confusing. Memory became a strange visitor, a distant and infrequent guest, and one that appeared and disappeared haphazardly and carelessly. It left its mess scrambled in her mind. But there was also humor. And humor was good; it offered light.

The story begins on Halloween in 1949 in a yellow taxicab on the way to St. Mary's Hospital in San Francisco. My mother is pregnant with me and she's already gone into labor. My father, a squeamish man who got light-headed over all matters regarding pain and blood, has just passed out in the front seat of the cab, hitting his head sharply on the dash. He is slumped over so he looks as though he is asleep. The cab driver is flying to the hospital, running red lights, passing cable cars, and sailing over the hilly roads at ridiculous speeds. Like a "rollacoasta," my mother would always say in her thick New York accent. At the emergency entrance they would take my mother and me one direction and my father the other. "With a beginning like that, how could you not have an interesting life?" That is a truth. I have lived a very interesting life.

My father was a corporate man. He was friendly and hard-working and, as a result, was quickly promoted up the ladder and that's how we ended up moving to Europe.

My father's words were true. Holland was a once-in-a-lifetime experience. We lived in a castle that had been converted into a grand hotel while my parents looked for a home. Left to our own devices, we children explored every inch of the hotel. We ordered room service whenever the mood struck. We explored the attics, ran through the manicured landscape playing hide-and-seek, fed the ducks and geese, chased sheep, and made friends with all the maids and bartenders.

My parents purchased a beautiful house with a thatched roof in the international section of Wassenaar, a small suburb of Den Haag. The children we would play with led international lives. Their parents were the heads of state and ambassadors to Holland from exotic countries like Rhodesia and the Ivory Coast. Once, on the way home from school, I saw four French kids beating up this tall, handsome young African boy. They were kicking him and calling him names. He wouldn't fight back so I dropped my books and jumped into the fight. I grew up in New York and the Mulman brothers had taught Eddie Seagull and me to be good fighters. Every day, on the way to school, the Mulmans would beat us up and take our lunch money. Soon, we got good enough to hold our own and the Mulmans took less and less of an interest in us. We learned through experience and I brought that "knuckle sandwich" experience with me into the fight.

There was no conversation because there was nothing to say. I couldn't speak French so I punched the biggest kid, a pug-ugly bully, on the side of the face. He fell to the ground and before he could get up, I kicked him in the stomach. He began to cry and these thugs took off running.

The young boy dusted himself off and with an exquisite Oxfordshire English accent, introduced himself to me. His name was Alan Piehl and his father was a king. He thanked me and told me he would not forget this gesture. He wondered, perhaps, if we could make an appointment to play together over the weekend. I told him I guessed so but I wasn't certain what an appointment meant. He laughed.

That night, his parents called mine to thank them for what I had done. My parents were confused and wanted to know exactly what I had done to warrant such attention. I told them it was no big deal. The following weekend, Alan made an appointment to play with me. He was driven to our house in a limousine and his driver waited while we played all day. With him, he brought a copy of *The Adventures of Robin Hood and His Merry Men* with an inscription inside the front cover thanking me for sticking up for him. It sits on my library shelf today.

We became blood brothers and sealed our oath by cutting our thumbs with a pocketknife and rubbing the blood together. It was an elaborate, secretive, childhood ceremony, finalized when we crossed piss in the secret "x" of brotherhood. Years later in college I would read that his family was murdered in a political coup in Zimbabwe.

Each year our international school would take several excursions into the industrial and rural areas surrounding Rotterdam and Amsterdam. They were fabulous adventures because they got me out of school. We toured a wooden shoe factory, a herring cannery where on a dare I slurped down a pickled herring, the Keukenhof Tulip Gardens, and a rope factory, which I admit was my favorite tour because they gave us all a small coil of rope.

In the fall of my fourth-grade year, rumor spread that one of our field trips would include a circus . . . not an ordinary circus but the gypsy circus of Romania, the Familia d'Romania, which managed to survive Hitler's genocide during World War II. It was a circus comprised of dwarves and midgets—a circus that was "our size." To be permitted to attend the event, it was required that a student be in good standing academically and have a parent in attendance at the circus.

Weeks before the circus came to town, I occupied my time by playing a game called Sheeny Boola, in which I played the part of a ringmaster, complete with my mother's top hat, a tuxedo too small for my father and too big for me, and a Zorro whip that was made from the rope our class got at the rope factory. It was taped to the handle of a broomstick. My brother, always, and my sister, whenever I could bribe her into playing with us, became whatever animals I needed them to be. I had a large cardboard box in my room that served as a lion's cage. I'd put my younger brother inside and fed him scraps of bread. He'd roar and I'd bring him out into the arena to perform a series of amazing feats. The three of us worked out a regular old circus act.

One afternoon I brought my father upstairs to watch our routine. After some pretty lame magic acts and pratfalls on the clown end of things, I put on the top hat and tuxedo and paraded my sister and brother around the room. We'd really polished up the act. I'd lead them in a circle and they'd whinny, rise up on their back hooves, turn about in a circle, and then stop parallel to each other while I'd stand on their backs. But the crowning glory of the act was when my brother would crawl around as fast as he could in a circle and I would jump over him. It was pure theatrics.

"Don't do it," my father warned, as I excitedly explained the upcoming performance to him. "You'll kick your brother in the head."

"We've done this a million times, Dad. Please? Please! Please!" My father relented and I promptly kicked my brother in the head and knocked him into la-la land. I was spanked and grounded from the upcoming circus.

I groveled. I played the subservient son. I shined all my father's dress shoes and was ungrounded. And just as quickly, I was grounded again after talking my brother into sliding down a wooden plank from the tree house that had a nail sticking through it. It was touch-and-go on a day-to-day basis, but by the week of the circus, it was clean sailing and I was off the hook.

By all parental measures, I'm certain the Familia d'Romania was a sleazy circus act and couldn't hold a candle to the big-top circus of Barnum and Bailey. The trapeze artists frequently missed their catches and the strong men didn't look so strong. The bareback riders were riding ponies, not real horses, and the clowns spilling out of a small car seemed logical because the performers were midgets. But we children of the International School were breathless.

The performers of the Familia d'Romania were our height and they were muscled and curved. The men had hair under their arms and bulges in their pants. The women had breasts, physiological elements that I did not completely appreciate until the fourth grade.

At one point in the performance, a volunteer was needed from the audience. The spotlight circled the arena and it stopped, as I knew it would, on Alan and me. I didn't give Alan a chance. I stood up and Zola came over to me and took my hand, leading me to the center of the ring. I could smell her perfume and I could see the tops of her breasts crowning over the black sequined outfit. Even with her top hat on, we were just about the same size. She smiled at me, gave me a giant hula-hoop, asked me to stand perfectly still, and then commanded a pack of dogs to jump from their platforms through the hoop. The crowd cheered and when I was finished she led me back to my seat and gave me a kiss on the cheek. Her face was dusted in golden sparkles.

My classmates thumped me on the back and said things I could not hear, and my parents, as my mother would recall, thought I was star struck and hormonally charged for the first time in my life. At that moment, I wanted to run away with Zola, Queen of the Lilliputians. It would have been such a good life.

Following the performance, I begged my parents to let us wander around the caravans to look at the circus folk. They agreed and probably followed close behind, out of sight, so I could entertain them with my star-struck lust. Alan and I ditched the other kids who had ridden to the circus with us and made our way through a labyrinth of clustered gypsy wagons looking for Zola. I wanted to tell Zola that I loved her and that I wanted to join the circus and travel with her. Her caravan was neatly painted white and had small flower boxes under the windows. Zola and the dogs were also crudely painted on the side of the caravan along with a picture of the Strongman bending a barbell in his teeth.

The curtains on the window were light blue, pulled back and tied so that we could actually see inside the caravan. The inside living space of Zola's home reminded me of a miniature dollhouse. There was a small seating area, an overhead wooden rack that held dishware, and a series of costumes hung on pegs against the far wall. A dog started barking, and the Strongman came into the doorframe, stepped down from the caravan, and asked us something. He wore heavy boots, tattered wool pants, and a tight, soiled, sleeveless T-shirt, and he was smoking a black cigarette. He repeated the question that was either in Dutch or Romanian. Close up, he frightened me. Alan nudged me. "I think we better go."

"Zola," I replied.

He looked at both of us and laughed. "Zola! Zola!" he barked. A moment later Zola appeared in a pink silk robe and joined us in the cool evening air. She was also smoking. She offered us cigarettes and said something to the Strongman and they laughed. She ran her fingers over my crew-cut hair and squeezed my arm. She said something to me and then called Alan "Swartza Pete" (Black Pete), the impish counterpart to St. Nicholas who appears in Dutch Christmas mythology. Without her makeup on, she looked tired. Her teeth were stained and she had large, dark bags under her eyes. She was older than my mother. The lines on her face were hard.

"Thank you," I said, and shook her hand. I shook the Strongman's hand, too. Alan and I hurried back to the front gate where we were supposed to meet my parents. When they arrived arm in arm, they were smiling. If they had watched me that night, they said nothing. It would have been easy to embarrass me. Instead, they just asked if we were ready to leave and I told them we were.

In the ninth grade, I would leave home and join a traveling carnival. But that is a story for another time. This story belongs to my mother and me. It was a shared memory; one that had deep roots that anchored her to a time when she was beautiful and young and my father was handsome and alive. And in this story, I am her son and I am in love with Zola, Queen of the Lilliputians, and sometimes, that's all a story needs to bring light into the world.

The Guy with the Big Ears

My mother and her very best ex-pat friend in Holland, Vera Kirchoffer, were very animated when I walked into the kitchen on my way out to the backyard to continue building the world's greatest tree house. I grabbed an apple from a French ceramic bowl and almost cleared their notice.

"We could have Jeff ride over on his bicycle and get his autograph," my mother remarked and Vera loved the idea.

"Ride where?" I asked.

"To the Kasteel," she replied. "We want you to do something for us."

Already I didn't like the sound of this because I had other things to do and felt suspiciously like this was a setup of disastrous proportion.

"Mom, I was going to work on the tree house. It's almost done."

"This is much bigger, Jeff. Something big, very big."

"Can't Sue do it?" The moment the question parted my lips I knew it was a ludicrous idea.

Sue, who was my older sister by a year, was not suited for any sort of adventure at the Kasteel. Our lives had been turned completely upside down when we moved to Holland. In a sense, we were living the classic American "rags to riches" narrative. My father, Jack, grew up in the small town of Hobart, Oklahoma. His own father, James Jefferson Metcalf, died when my father was only eleven years old, leaving behind his wife, my grandmother

Birdie Mae, with four little kids to raise. It was a scrabble-rock existence.

My mother's family grew up in Staten Island. Her mother, my grandmother Rosy, worked as a switchboard operator, and my grandfather, Walter, was the superintendent of a tenement building on Silver Lake Road. One day we're living in New York and the next day, as my grandmother would say, we were living the "Life of Riley." Now my father worked for Standard Oil and my mother was a full-time wife and socialite in a very elite inner circle of ambassadors' and diplomats' wives from a wide range of foreign countries with exotic names like Rhodesia, Lebanon, Morocco, Belgium, Germany, and Luxembourg.

"No, it can't be Sue," my mother replied. "We need you."

"Why?"

"Because Clark Gable's at the Kasteel with Kay Spreckles. Vera read about it in the *Herald Tribune*."

"He just finished a picture and he's staying at the Kasteel. Maybe he's in the suite we lived in when we first arrived," my mother added as though that might make the bell ring for me.

"I don't know who he is."

"He's Clark Gable, the MOVIE STAR," Vera added like she was certain her own miscreant children would have understood immediately.

"Mom, do you know him?"

"Of course not, dear. We just want you to ride your bike over, take a piece of paper, and see if you can get him to sign an autograph."

"One for each of us," Vera added handing me a couple of pieces of stationery. "Don't you know who he is?"

"No."

Adults were strange to me.

If I didn't understand who Clark Gable was when my mother asked me, why would I know who he was three seconds later when Vera asked me?

"Here," my mother said, take this as a little something and she handed me five guilders. I nearly protested but gladly grabbed the cash and headed out the door in search of the guy with the big ears.

When I arrived at the Kasteel, I rode my bike to the back of the hotel and placed it in a rack where the hotel staff parked. I knew a great number of the staff by name because we'd lived in the Kasteel when we first arrived in Holland.

My first trip would be to the bar where I hoped "Hank the Bartender" was still working. While living in the Kasteel, Hank had become our best friend. He spoke very good English and he liked the Metcalf kids. An after-school ritual would be to stop by the bar, pick up some stale bread, and feed the ducks and geese spread out on the Kasteel's meandering streams and ponds. Then we'd collect together, go into the bar, sit at the table, and order peanuts and have a cold Coke. All of this would be charged to our room, something beyond our wildest dreams. And then, after we'd done our homework, we'd all retreat to the dining room and order anything off of the menu. Anything. Whatever this new job was that my father had fallen into, we liked it.

Hank was in the bar when I arrived. He greeted me, asked how my family was, and plunked a cold Coke down at the end of the bar. I climbed up on the barstool and took a large glug of the soda. He brought some peanuts over and set them in front of me and slid a tiny cup of maraschino cherries and some cocktail napkins off to the side.

"The Kasteel is not so exciting since your family has left," he said with a big smile. "There are not many children here. Just one now."

"Is he an American kid?" I asked.

"Yes."

"A girl or a boy?"

"A boy. I think your age."

"Do you know what school he'll be going to?" I asked. My curiosity was busting out in a big way. We were currently attending the International School and there weren't a large number of Americans attending the school so this was important. Being the friend to a new kid and bringing him into the fold carried great weight in the hierarchy of the schoolyard.

"What's his name?"

"It is a funny name. I can only remember the Dutch word, 'kazemat.' Do you know it?"

"No."

"I thought you were learning Dutch. That's what your mother said."

"Mostly I've learned to swear."

"That can be important."

"Do you know where the boy is going to live?"

"Oh, no, they won't live here. His father is very important. They live in Hollywood."

"Why are they here, then?" I asked wondering why anybody would come to Holland just to visit.

"The young boy is with his father. He's a movie star and he's very famous."

This was just about too much for me to comprehend. The Kasteel de Wittenberg was crawling with movie stars. How was I supposed to find the right one and get him to sign a piece of paper?

"He's outside with his mother. His father is talking to the news. If you want, I will walk you outside."

"Does he have big ears?"

"Very big. Why?"

"My mom sent me over to get some papers signed with his name. I need some paper."

Hank brought me some stationery from the Kasteel and then walked me out to the back garden of the hotel. The guy with the big ears was getting his picture taken by a bunch of newspaper types. There was a beautiful lady standing off to the side, and next to her, a kid who looked about my age.

"Jeff, I must go back to the bar. When he is done giving his photographs, he will probably sign your papers."

I waited. The kid saw me. I smiled and so did he. He had a Little League T-shirt on so I knew he was American. The guy with the big ears did a lot of smiling and sure had a lot of pictures taken of him. Pretty soon, I got bored and walked over to him. Everybody seemed surprised.

"Hi, I'm Jeff and my mother told me to get you to sign this. I'm not supposed to leave until you do." I handed him the stationery. Then the cameras really started clicking. The man with the big ears started laughing and tousled my hair, which I hated.

"I'll tell you what, Jeff, I'm a bit busy right now but why don't you go over there and play with my son. His name is Bunker. When I'm done, you can have lunch with us and I'd be happy to sign this for your mother."

"Okay," I said, and went directly over to meet Bunker Gable. Kazemat. Bunker. Of course.

His mom's name was Kay. She was very beautiful and reminded me of my Aunt Marge who was married to my mother's brother, Bill. Kay said it was okay if we played together as long as we didn't leave the Kasteel property and we returned to their suite in an hour.

I took Bunker under my wing and we took off on a great adventure. I showed him all the secret back passageways in the hotel, got a big bag of bread to feed the ducks, took him into the bar where Hank poured us some leftover champagne, snuck into the cold-storage food lockers where we gorged on ice cream, got in a half-sunk row boat and played pirates, threw rocks at squirrels, and put him on the back of my bike where we rode along the bike path to a sweet shop to get some candy. We lost track of time. By the time we got back onto the property and headed into the bar to see what was going on, Hank was excited.

"The house detectives have been looking for the two of you. What happened?"

"Nothing. We were just playing."

"Come, we must go to the front desk."

We followed Hank to the front desk and then the manager took us both up to the guy with the big ears' suite. When he opened the door, he wasn't happy looking.

"Where the hell have you been?" he asked Bunker. "You scared the hell out of us. We thought you'd drowned or been kidnapped!"

"We were just playing," Bunker offered weakly. His mother entered the room and ran over and hugged him. She looked over at me and then back to Bunker. "How long did I tell you that you could play with him?"

"An hour." That was the truth, I heard it myself.

"How long do you think you've been gone?"

"An hour," he said, shrugging his shoulders.

"Over three hours," she cried. "We were afraid something horrible had happened." She started to cry and because I felt so bad, I started to cry. Plus, I was afraid that I was going to get a good spanking for being gone so long. Finally, the guy with the big ears calmed everybody down. He ordered room service and once we'd eaten, he told me he'd have his car brought around and he'd take me home. I told him it was okay, that I'd ridden home from the Kasteel in the dark a number of times. He insisted.

Before I left the room, he ripped a piece of paper off of his desk and signed it. "Here kid, this is for you." I folded it up and put it in my pocket. He only signed one piece of paper but I didn't have the nerve to ask him for another.

The driver placed my bike in the trunk of his car. The guy with the big ears and I sat in the back together. He asked me about my family and then I asked him what he did for a living. He told me he was in the motion picture business. He made movies. I asked him a bunch of questions. He really seemed like a nice guy.

When we pulled down the driveway of Koninginneweg 2, I told him he could just let me off here and I'd be fine. He wouldn't have any of that so he took me directly to the front door and rang the doorbell. I was in deep trouble and it would only get deeper if he hung around and told my parents about me making his wife sick with worry.

My mother opened the door and was about to launch into me for getting home so late when she saw the guy with the big ears and became a deaf mute. Dumfounded. My father was directly behind her. I think she was in some sort of trance at the time. My father stuck his hand out and greeted the guy with the big ears, "Hello, I'm Jack Metcalf and this is my wife, Mary." My mother mumbled something unintelligible.

"It's a pleasure to meet you, Jack. I'm Clark Gable. I've already met your son, Jeff. He spent the day playing with my son, Bunker. I brought him home. It was getting late."

"The least I can do is to offer you a drink, Clark. Would you like to join us for a cocktail?"

"I'd love to," the guy with big ears replied and he walked into our house and I went upstairs to the room I shared with my brother to see if anything interesting had happened while I was gone.

Magpie

The difficulty in living in the Netherlands as an eight-year-old boy was not what one might expect; the absence of friends, the lack of common language, a radical departure in dietary habits, leaving family behind in New York, being the new kid in an international school where most of your classmates were upper-crust from around the globe, or trying to learn French as a third grader. The problem was more troublesome. It was much more dire than that.

As ex-pats, we had little live communication with the world we left behind. Which meant, of course, no access to a radio where I could listen to the 1957 World Series. Our only real source of information was from the *Herald Tribune*, and short of reporting the scores in minimalistic sports reporting, it had little to offer. By the time one received a *Herald Tribune*, the news was already a couple of days old.

I was a hard-core Yankee fan and I knew they'd clinched the American League series and had a berth in the World Series against the Milwaukee Braves of the National League. Duh! It was expected, wasn't it? But beyond that, it was like living in a time warp of sorts. The first game was played and three or four days later I'd hear about it when the old man got the paper and relayed the score to me. That paper wasn't going to touch my mitts until the old man had read everything he needed to read. And that could mean twenty minutes on the short end. So, I'd retreat to my bedroom, spread the baseball cards out on the floor, draw up the batting order for both teams, and imagine who would be the opening pitchers and what the starting lineup would look like.

You knew the score already because the Yankees were the Yankees. The Yankees won the first game at Yankee Stadium 3–2. You were empowered because you could see into the future and you could live without the very thing you wanted most, a play-by-play narration of the first game because the Yankees won.

In this world without radio, you got to speculate whom "the Perfessor," Casey Stengel, was going to have on the mound. It had to be Whitey Ford and you guessed he'd go up against Warren Spahn. The rest of the Yankee lineup was a cinch: Bauer, McDougald, Mantle, Skowron, Berra, Carey, Coleman, Kubek, and Ford.

The Braves, on the other hand, really didn't matter because you were a Yankee fan. But, and this is one of the dark mysteries of the universe to you, the Braves have a couple of players on the roster that you actually admire and secretly would like to see jump to the Yankees' lineup: Warren Spahn, Wes Covington, Hank Aaron. To say this out loud in the old neighborhood would have been an unpardonable sin of great consequence. Game number one was a forgone conclusion, and game number two would be the same. The opening games were played at Yankee Stadium, and when it came to the World Series in Yankee Stadium, nobody beat the Yanks on their own turf. I imagined the Yankees at 2–0 heading to Milwaukee and returning back with a 4–1 series and another World Series title. End of story.

I almost died when I got the *Herald Tribune* and discovered the Yankees lost the second home game 4–2. The third game of the series let the Braves know who was in charge when the Yankees clobbered them at home in County Stadium 12–5. The Yankees lost game four in a demoralizing, extra-inning win by the Braves of 7–5 and then lost the next game 1–0 before returning to Yankee Stadium.

In my world, this was utterly unthinkable. The Yankees behind 3–2 in the World Series? Secretly, I began to wonder if I'd jinxed the Yankees by liking Spahn, Covington, and Aaron. This waiting for a three- to four-day-old paper was unbearable . . . truly beyond the pale and reasonable expectation of any baseball fan. Game six was a squeaker and the Yankees managed to claw their way to a 3–2 win. Game seven would be played on October tenth, a mere twenty-one days before my birthday. I swore that I would forgo any birthday present if the gods would let the Yanks win the final game of the series.

The final game was played on a Thursday and I would not know the result until Monday, October fourteenth. As always, I would have to wait until my father returned from work with the paper. The moment I heard his car ramble up the gravel driveway, I rushed out to greet him. His face betrayed nothing. I took his leather briefcase from the back seat and carried it into the house for him. Normally, he'd give me the score if I wanted it but today he offered nothing. At most, my father had a mild interest in baseball and did not know of the weight and guilt I'd been carrying on my shoulders.

"Dad," I asked, trying to sound very casual, "who won the World Series?"

"Oh," he replied, looking at the *Herald Tribune* folded under his arm, "I haven't even glanced at the paper. Here, take it."

"Thanks, dad . . . thanks." I promised to bring the paper down to the living room after I'd had a chance to read it. My emotions were all over the map. I'd worked out every scenario in my head and I was convinced, given the odds, the dangers, and the unpredictability and resiliency of the Braves, that the Yankees would ultimately still triumph. It boiled down to the following three indisputable arguments: (1) the Yankees were the Yankees; (2) the final game of the series was being played in Yankee Stadium; and (3) they won in 1956 beating the Brooklyn Dodgers 9–zip in the seventh game. In an away game, no less. So, who was in the catbird seat? It had been written.

After reading the sports headlines and discovering the Yankees had lost at home, I was inconsolable. I cried like a little baby and there was no way I could stop myself. How could the Yankees do such a thing? I was thousands of miles away and I'd counted on them. It was going to be my birthday present. Was that too much to ask?

I didn't eat much for dinner, feigning a loss of appetite, and when I announced that the Yankees had lost the series there was hardly a shrug of anybody's shoulders. My brother was too young to care, my sister was thinking about becoming a nun, which was fine by me, and both my parents were invested in conversation about a huge Halloween costume party they would be throwing in a couple of weeks.

My suffering was invisible. I might have been depressed if we had known then what we know now about the word. It was so bad, in fact, that for the next two weeks I did not bring home a single note from my third-grade teacher requiring my parents' signature acknowledging that they had read and understood completely, in one way or the other, that their son was a complete cock-up. When no notes appeared for two weeks straight, my father began to worry.

Heading toward the end of October, my father asked if I wanted to walk with him along the tram tracks that ran parallel to our home into town to pick up some pastries at our favorite shop. Just the two of us, so I jumped at the chance. I loved that private time with him. We'd just walk and sometimes we'd talk and other times we wouldn't. This time, however, he asked me what was wrong before we'd settled into our gait.

I told him everything and it came out as a bundle of word spill, not well articulated, I'm certain, but he was an intelligent man and I knew he could sort it all out. After some thought, he said, "Sometimes things don't turn out the way you expect them to, Jeff. It's part of life."

Seriously, that was the best he could offer? A moment later, perhaps sensing my great and utter disappointment, he added, "It's only a game and there is always next year."

I sulked into the pastry shop and was going to refuse to eat anything but the smells were beyond anything I could resist. We both had a favorite pastry with apple and orange in a circular twisted bun. My father had stiff coffee and I had a half hot chocolate and half coffee mix.

On the return trip home, my father asked me how my arm was doing. I obliged him by picking up perfect rocks and chucking them as far as I possibly could. I imagined myself as Mickey Mantle, throwing from center field to home base. He was clearly impressed. In front of us, a fair distance and off to the side of the track, a magpie was scavenging a rodent carcass.

"Do you think I could hit it from here, dad?"

"Why would you want to do that?"

"Because they're robbers. They steal eggs from other nests."

"It's their nature."

"But do you think I could hit it from here?"

"It's a long shot, Jeff. Don't do it unless you understand what's involved. There are consequences to everything we do."

My dad could be like that sometimes. Mystical. I actually wasn't that interested in hitting the magpie so it was no big deal. I was pretty certain I wouldn't get close, but in that split second between the thought and the act, I let go. The rock was clearly off target until the magpie suddenly spooked and took flight, aligning itself perfectly with the oncoming rock. There was a horrific cry, a flap of feathers, and the magpie dropped to the ground. It lay there, wing broken, groveling in a circle. There was no sense of accomplishment in the moment. It scared me. I looked at my father for reassurance of some sort. It was an accident. I mean, how could I have possibly knocked a bird out of the sky?

"I didn't mean to, Dad."

"You threw the rock, Jeff."

"I didn't think I could hit it. Not from here."

"But you did. What are you planning to do?"

"Take it home and fix it."

By then, we'd closed the distance and I could see droplets of blood on the magpie's splendid wing. I grabbed my father's hand.

"I didn't mean to do it, honestly."

"You need to put it out of its misery, Jeff."

"You mean kill it?"

"Yes," my father said quietly. "It's suffering."

"I can't. I don't know how," I cried and then begged, "Please, Dad . . . couldn't you do this?"

"I could but I won't, Jeff. It's your responsibility."

I was beside myself and I pleaded with him but my father was recalcitrant.

"How? What should I do?"

"Use a stick or a rock."

I picked up a stout stick from the side of the track and stood over the magpie. Its beak cawed open and shut and it made a desperate, wounded cry. It attempted to scuttle away. I looked back at my father. He nodded his head. I swung the stick down on the magpie. At the last moment the magpie moved and I cracked its broken wing. It flipped over on its back. I was crying and my father was blurring away. I needed him to help me do this. His voice was soft and firm.

"You need to finish this, son."

I swung again and this time I crushed its skull. Fragments of small bone and flesh lay splayed against the gravel. My father came to my side and took the stick out of my hand. I buried my head in his jacket and sobbed. After a short time when I had settled down enough, he spoke to me softly.

"It's okay. Let's go home."

Jungle Dream

I couldn't shake this one. It followed me, night after night for two months, and then it disappeared just as suddenly as it appeared. There was nothing I could do and I didn't want to talk with anyone about it. Because in the talking, I feared it might become.

How does such a dream find you? I was far too young for such matters, for such ghosts, and the staggering weight of this particular dream was noticed by my parents. I had dark circles under my eyes. I wasn't sleeping and I would often wake up screaming until one of my parents entered the room and held me until I settled down.

I was ten years old when the girl first stood up in the forest and smiled at me. I waved at her and returned the smile. She waved back and then bent into the lush green foliage to retrieve something. I was point man on patrol with a group of other soldiers and looked briefly over my shoulder to see if they, too, had noticed her. I can still see them clearly now. They smiled back at me in acknowledgment of this beautiful child.

In this dream, I was not a small, ten-year-old boy. I was a nineteen-year-old infantryman in the United States Army, in a tropical landscape unknown to me by anything I could imagine or recall from the numerous *National Geographic* magazines that filled our family study.

What struck me about my "older" self was how fit and trim I was; how I had grown into my body and, in recollection of this dream at nineteen, how much I had physically morphed into the "dream" self.

When I left home for college I was seventeen years old. I was raw and unsettled. Halfway around the world, an ugly war was escalating at an alarming rate. Through television, I would, in the course of five years, witness race riots, the death of Malcolm X, John F. Kennedy, Martin Luther King Jr., and a steady stream of caskets returning from Vietnam. In my first year of college, I would enroll in ROTC intent on defending the country from the great communist menace and the collapse of democracy through the "domino effect." I was ready to do my part and if I had to give up my life, I would do so without hesitation.

And then, I read. And asked questions. And demonstrated. I would be watched and photographed. I would develop a political consciousness and it would save my soul.

I did not become a second lieutenant and I withdrew from the ROTC program. I did not join the National Guard to stay out of the draft. I was at odds with my country and nothing associated with Vietnam or our political scene made any sense at all.

I was vocal in my beliefs. I was told by one of my parents' friends, an FBI agent, that I should not be so visible. In 1972, before I graduated from the university, my draft status had suddenly changed. I was categorized as 1-A by the Selective Service, a "registrant available for military service." I would challenge the Selective Service in court on three separate issues and lose on all of them. On October 27, 1972, four days before my twenty-third birthday, I would receive a letter from the Selective Service system informing me that my final appeal had been declined and that I effectively would be drafted into the United States Army.

That very same night, the dream revealed itself. Informed perhaps by all the images I had witnessed on television and over countless evening broadcasts of a senseless war, the features were sharp and focused. I understood the dream.

The girl was no longer a girl. Now, she was a young woman about the same age as I and she was determined. She wore black silk pajamas, a silk scarf, and woven straw hat. The smile was not at all innocent. It was angry and defiant. The girl bent over and disappeared into the undergrowth just as she had done when I was a young boy. When she stood back up, she hefted a hand-held rocket, leveled it at us, and fired at point-blank range.

Hush Puppies

I remember very little about the eighth grade that I liked. In fact, I have only a handful of memories scattered about my landscape that I'd care to remember. The new kid again, starting over, dropped into school mid-year, from Saudi Arabia to Pershing Junior High School, Houston, Texas, 1963, living in the Stella Link Apartments on a busy street facing heavy traffic.

The bedroom I shared with my brother faced a large neon Star of David from the Jewish delicatessen and it blinked steadily all day and all night. Since our room had no curtains, it was like the Chinese water torture, a constant distraction, a reminder that we were without a permanent home, my father looking for work after a splendid job in the Middle East.

Our furniture, clothing, toys, kitchen wares, washer and dryer, television, everything one needs to make a home—had somehow in the course of transatlantic shipping, been lost on a slow boat to Hong Kong and would not catch up to us for over a year. Our life at the Stella Link Apartments became a year of Spartan and minimalistic living. Hollow-core doors served as study desks and platforms for our bed mattresses. Closet doors, the hardware removed, became coffee and dining room tables. We were known as the kids whose parents had no furniture. Strangers in a strange land, so it seemed.

It took me some time to understand the language of Texans. Before moving around overseas, I'd grown up in New York, where language was a weapon and could be used to cut, slash, and insult. Texans spoke in dreamy, lazy, thickly drenched, almost slow-witted rhythms. And though it was clear to me who sounded funny, I was often asked by a group of girls to say certain words like "coffee," "quarter," and "oil." Because I wanted so badly to fit in, I would oblige them at my own expense.

To fit in. That's what it was all about in the eighth grade. To be a part of the whole. Because I didn't fit in, I'd try to disappear in a throng of students, a phantom roaming the halls between classes. I wanted to be a kid who didn't stand out, who blended in. Not too much to hope for, to ask.

I was a careful student of camouflage, paid close attention to the fashion of Pershing Junior High School and when my birthday rolled around, I gave my mother a very detailed clothing list, things I would absolutely need to build my style and help me become part of the scene. My desert boots, long since dead and stashed in the closet with their soles hanging out like a panting dog's tongue, had been my last connecting link to my friends in Saudi Arabia. We all wore desert boots. We lived in a desert. It made sense. I would need something else.

Bass Weejuns. Oxblood. Penny loafers. This was the epitome of fashion. Anything else wouldn't do and although I had never been particularly conscious of wearing the "right" things before, this was a different game. These Texans paid attention to such details, to fashion. If I was going to be in this game I needed to climb on board. The only thing standing between the blending of a world I wasn't part of and a world I wanted to be part of, was my mother. Her dramatic flair for clothing made her stand out wherever she went. This, I knew, would always be a problem between us.

Long before fashion consultants made a fancy living by matching people's clothing to the color auras surrounding them, my mother was practicing the art to a heightened level. My colors were rust and gold. As she explained, they went with the month of

October, my birth month. To this day I can't wear anything with the colors rust and gold and my sister can't drink red wine because her colors were burgundy and maroon.

In the kid rotation, it was my turn for a pair of shoes and I knew exactly what they would be. To be certain there could be no mistake in the transaction, I drew my mother a picture of what the Weejuns looked like, including the color, size, the store where she could find the best price, and I went so far as to give her the name of the salesman who would help her, who was actually holding a pair of Weejuns at Sharpstown Mall with my name on them, and then I waited.

In the days that followed, my imagination ran wild, freestyle, waxed in fantasy; I could see myself styling down the hall, my new oxblood Weejuns, slippery leather bottoms gliding past petite Cindi Braxton, headband pulling her golden hair off her alabaster face, green eyes, perfect teeth, pleated McStewart kilt, small breasts. And she would want to know who the new guy was with the oxblood Weejuns. I had faith in my mother.

The shoebox sat dead center on my bed. It wasn't a Weejun box. I knew what they looked like. There must have been a horrific mistake; perhaps my mother had accidentally placed my brother's shoes on my bed. I opened the box delicately as though it might be attached to a trip wire on a live bomb. When I peeled back the tissue, I was crushed. Instead of Weejuns, my mother had bought me a pair of bright red, Japanese lantern red, suede Hush Puppies. I was dead. Period.

I grabbed the box and stormed into the kitchen where my mother was cooking dinner. I babbled like a madman. "These aren't Weejuns, MOM! These aren't even close! I can't wear these. I'll get beat up. How could you do this to me?"

"Settle down Jeff. I went to the mall and looked at the Weejuns. They were seventeen dollars and I wasn't about to spend that kind of money on shoes for you when you're growing so fast."

"You could have bought them a size too large. I could have stuffed cotton in the toes and I could grow into them."

"What's the problem with them? There's nothing wrong with those shoes. They're red, they'll fit you, and they were on sale."

"Jesus mom . . ."

"Watch your language, young man!"

"Kids don't wear Hush Puppies, Mom. Old men do. Old men who wear their pants up around their neck. Old men like Mr. Weingartener from the deli. Those are the kind of guys who wear Hush Puppies. The kids at Pershing Junior High School don't wear these. I'll be laughed out of school."

"There is nothing wrong with them! It's the only pair of shoes you're getting and who cares what the kids at Pershing think! Make a fashion statement. Start your own trend. Be a leader and not a follower."

"I care Mom! I care! Doesn't that mean anything to you?" I was working myself into a frenzy. "Fashion statement! What this fashion statement says is: Nerd. Dweeb. Geek. Spastic. Is that what you want people to think of me? I'll go barefooted before I wear these, Mom, I swear. Somebody will kick the snot out of me."

There was a moment of silence between us, that space where a kid crosses a line and offers the CHALLENGE, the THREAT. And when the gauntlet is thrown down, there is only one parental response and it is invited and understood by both parties.

"There are people all over the world who would be happy just to have a pair of nice shoes like those."

And then I said it. "Well, if they need shoes so badly, why don't we make them happy and mail these off to them right now?"

In my room, I had plenty of time to think things over. Working the angles over and over again, I still came up with the same conclusion. My mother was planning to get rid of me and the red Hush Puppies would be the cause. But the fear of having to deal with my father when he got home almost made me retract what I'd said to my mother, but not quite.

There is nothing worse than coming home after an unsuccessful day pounding the pavement, looking for a job, and having to deal with one of your own miscreants. However, I was resolute. I would not wear those Hush Puppies. My father looked tired. He shut the door to my bedroom and sat on my brother's bed.

"Want to tell me what happened with your mother?"

I explained the situation, I told him about the map I'd drawn for mom, the importance of fitting in, how wearing the red Hush Puppies might actually be dangerous to my health. I told him how I'd exploded at mom and she back at me. He listened patiently, every so often nodding his head to let me know he was in the moment. When I'd finished weaving my story he only had one thing to say.

"They can't be that bad, can they?"

"Close your eyes, Dad."

I quickly slipped off my slippers and pushed my feet into the Hush Puppies. To be honest, they didn't feel that bad. But the color? Jesus, no way! When my father opened his eyes, his expression said it all. I knew he had to back my mother up, that was just the way it was with him, but his expression was clearly behind me.

"They're not that bad," he said. It was an exhausted voice.

"Would you wear them, Dad? Honestly, would you be caught dead in these shoes?"

"It's just not my kind of shoe, Jeff."

I had him over a barrel and I wasn't about to let him go. I'd had more time to prepare and the day would ultimately go to me.

"It's not my kind of shoe, either, Dad. Would you wear these?" I looked him squarely in the eyes.

To say "yes" would incriminate him. I had my father in a beautiful position. His answer was barely audible. "No. No, I wouldn't. I'll talk to your mother."

Out of sight behind the kitchen door, I listened to my father and mother fight about the shoes. My father was clearly on my side. "A guy can't wear shoes like that. He'll be the laughing stock of the school."

This was good stuff and I couldn't have done any better myself.

But, in the end, my mother won out. She told my father how much Weejuns cost, which drew a whistle from him, mentioned the fact the Hush Puppies were half the price, heaped on a bit about mom and dad raising kids who should value the inside of a person and not their outward appearance, vis-à-vis, clothes don't make the person, etc. I could tell the old man was up against the ropes. Then she delivered the knockout punch, "And you know, with you still out of work we've just got to watch our budget." My father was out cold.

I resolved to make the best of it. Thursday morning I got up early. I gobbled breakfast, showered, and got myself dressed. I put on the red Hush Puppies, more for my father than for any other reason. If I walked to school in the dark, nobody would notice the shoes and if I hung around by the shop annex until the bell rang, I could possibly sneak into class without being noticed. Lunch would be a problem, but I had time to think of some way to make it without being discovered.

Matters were going pretty well. A couple of kids were smoking out by the shop class and didn't pay any attention to me. Six minutes until the bell would ring and then it happened. Chuck Logee, the only seventeen-year-old eighth grader in the history of Pershing Junior High, drove up in his car and parked about five yards away from where I was hiding. Chuck was a bully, had his own car, and was one mean son-of-a-bitch. What he lacked in brains, he made up for in cruelty. I nodded my head at him and he just stared at me. A guy like me didn't nod my head to a guy like Chuck Logee. We had gym class together and several times I watched him give "swirlees" to the weaker guys by pushing their heads into the toilet and flushing it. We also had woodshop class together and while most of us were making shoe-shine boxes for our dads or jewelry boxes for our mothers, Chuck was making a full-blown gun cabinet with glass doors, something he'd started on a couple of years earlier and might complete this year. He knew the shop teacher pretty well and even called him by his first name.

He moved in on me. "So, where'd the Ayrab kid get them pimp shoes?" He walked up to me and scuffed the red suede of my shoes with his leather biker boots.

"My mom. You know how moms can be." I tried desperately to be casual and cool.

"Those are faggot shoes. Only a faggot would wear them."

I said nothing. He grabbed me by the front of my shirt and shoved me up against the wall. "Faggot. How about a little faggot kiss?"

A crowd was gathering. Chuck Logee was choking me and just when I thought I was going to pass out, I unleashed a sucker punch. I caught Chuck on the side of his head and he dropped straight to the ground. Stunned more than anything else, he came up swinging but I'd clearly surprised him. He caught me across the bridge of the nose and it started bleeding but I got in several solid licks before the fight got broken up. Chuck Logee had lost face. He threatened to kill me if he ever saw me again, but I didn't back down. And we would hook it out two more times before the end of the year but he couldn't hurt me. I was beyond Chuck Logee.

I had gym before lunch. We went swimming for P.E. and the cold water felt soothing on my face. I was beginning to relax when the school P.A. system interrupted our class. The principal called for our attention and made the announcement that President John F. Kennedy had been shot in Dallas. A few students cheered, but most of us hung to the side of the pool stunned. School was dismissed early and I walked home feeling lower than I'd ever felt in my life.

When I got home, my mother was sitting in front of the television with a handkerchief held up to her nose. My father, who had flown out earlier that morning, called from Dallas where only moments before he had seen the Kennedys and Governor

Connally riding in the motorcade. Like the rest of the nation, a part of me died that day. It wasn't until the middle of dinner that my mom noticed my bruises.

"What happened to you?"

"I wore my new shoes to school, got in a fight, and President Kennedy got shot."

Later that evening, after everybody went to bed, I carried my Hush Puppies into the kitchen. I took a large cast-iron frying pan, poured cooking oil into it and turned on the burner. When the pan got good and hot I sautéed my shoes. My mother came running into the kitchen. The smell of burning rubber made my eyes water. If the truth were known, I was crying. I was crying for myself, my father being out of work, for the death of John F. Kennedy, and being stuck in Texas.

My mother turned off the burner, took a pair of barbecue tongs and lifted my shoes out of the pan, and dropped them into a garbage pail. She wrapped her arm around me and walked me back to my bedroom. For a moment she sat on the bed and just held me, and then, she took a deep breath, as though she were going to speak, exhaled, and started crying. I had never heard my mother cry like this before, but as I grew older, I would come to know that sound as my own.

Silkies

My maternal grandmother, Rosy Dugan, was a storyteller. She would never think of herself as such, but to any of us in the family, it went without challenge or question. She was my favorite relative. I think I tell stories because of her.

My mother called it a "gift" and she, in turn, inherited the ability to hold spell over any crowd she performed in front of. My mother's stories blended the fiction and fact of our lives in such seamless and shameless narrative that it was often difficult to sort the two out. I inherited the gift and have, in turn, passed it on to our children, Bailey and John, who in their own right are marvelous storytellers.

I remember with a great deal of fondness living with Rosy and Pops in their cramped, two-bedroom apartment on Staten Island before leaving for Europe and the Middle East. We were squished and compressed, living, it seemed, on top of and under each other, but there are good memories there. Rosy was a devout Catholic and every Sunday she would cook corned beef and cabbage and we'd feed the parish priest and, it seemed to me, half the building.

The interior of the apartment had no dining room so our meals were taken outside of the apartment in a long passageway where a large, solid-core door had been placed on top of saw horses and covered with a brightly colored oil cloth. Surrounding the table were a series of mismatched chairs, many of them repaired by my grandfather. Some would sway under the girth of the guests when they sat at the Sunday table.

It was at this table that my fascination with Ireland began. When my grandmother determined that everybody was "goodly fed," she would hold court. Her tales of Ireland were mythological and mysterious, steeped in the folklore of land and sea. There were, of course, many stories of leprechauns and banshees, the tale of the Blarney Stone, but most seductive to me were the tales of silkies, those mermaids and mermen who inhabited the bodies of bright-eyed seals and beckoned to seafarers and landlubbers alike.

The 1950s was the zenith of radio and although I was mesmerized by the *Lone Ranger*, *The Shadow*, and *The Adventures of Superman*, they could not begin to scratch the surface of my grandmother's tales. A silkie seemed, in many respects, much more plausible. Part human, part seal with the ability to shed their skin and transform into the human form was a powerful elixir for me. There was not a single trip on the Staten Island Ferry from the St. George Terminal on Bay Street to Manhattan that I didn't stand, upper deck, rail side, pressed against strangers, peering into the depths of dark green water with a vigilant eye for silkies. A chorus from my grandmother and parents warning me that I'd catch my death of cold if I didn't bundle up meant nothing to me. I was not even discouraged by my older sister, who actually did know everything, as she pointed out that not a single case of silkie sightings had ever occurred anywhere other than Ireland and Scotland. My argument, certainly in the world of the silkie logic, was simple: If a silkie was in love with an Irish immigrant, might she not be compelled to follow him across the ocean, emerge from the water, shed her skin, and bury it safely until she found that man she loved?

One evening, shortly before my family left the United States to live in Holland, we gathered for one last dinner in my grandparents' hallway for dinner. The clan had gathered to officially hear "the announcement" that we'd be leaving the country. Although it was supposed to be a guarded secret, I suspect all of them already knew. My mother began by retelling the story about how the decision had been made.

"So I said to Jack," she offered, a martini in one hand and a cigarette in the other, "'Grab a quarter out of your pocket and flip. Heads we go. Tails we stay.'" Conversation stopped and my mother used the silence for dramatic effect.

Somebody from the crowd said, "You can't be serious? That's how you made the decision?"

My mother nodded her head.

"'Flip the coin, Jack.'"

My mother mimed the flipping of the quarter into the air. The grownups, mouths agape, followed the imaginary quarter as it ascended into the heavens, held for brief pause before descending back to earth and into my mother's palm where she flipped it over on her forearm and announced, "Heads!"

Our relatives and friends gasped and clapped. She, too, was indeed a gifted storyteller.

Cigarette and cigar smoke filled the hallway. Pros and cons of the move were debated. The cousins crowded together on the floor and listened carefully to the adults. Gael, my favorite cousin, looked at me as though we were moving to Borneo where wild men would cannibalize us. My heart sank. We were truly leaving New York and truly leaving my grandmother's table.

As we left, my grandmother pulled me close to her and whispered, "You'll be on a great ship crossing the ocean. Keep your eyes open for silkies. Promise me now!" I promised. "And, who knows, you might someday make it to the Emerald Isle."

To leave the warmth of my grandmother and her stories behind seemed unbearable. For the next nine years, as we lived a fascinating life residing in Europe and the Middle East, silkies would give way to the exotic landscapes which carried their own particular weight of mythology and intrigue.

The dream of traveling to Ireland in search of silkies would remain submerged beneath my own topography for twenty years, but my grandmother had indeed planted that seed.

White Goats and Black Bees

It would take over twenty years for me to convert the rich tales of Ireland told to me by my grandmother Rosy into my first visit to the Emerald Isle in 1977.

Northern Ireland was Protestant unionist country, loyal to the United Kingdom, while southern Ireland was comprised of Catholic nationalists, almost all uniformly in favor of a united Ireland. It's an old and tired story; a divided country fueled by deep-seated religious, political, economic, and national differences, and punctuated by unnecessary violence. A general IRA ceasefire had been negotiated but ultimately failed, along with several unsuccessful attempts at power sharing between the Catholics and Protestants. Scotland, my friends had argued, might be a safer place to visit, but Scotland was not where my clan hailed from. We hailed from Ireland and none of my friends had ever "sat to sup" with my grandmother Rosy at the height of her story-telling days.

Since Northern Ireland seemed always a few degrees away from boiling over, and the violent tactics of the IRA were unpredictable, Ireland was not a top tourist destination. Fortunately for me, at the time a fourth-year high school English teacher, Ireland was within the range of affordability.

In June I would depart for Ireland with no itinerary, an open airline ticket, a rucksack, a hopeless sense of the romantic, the river's tooth of stories from Rosy, and a letter of invitation from author Donald Grant, formerly a top correspondent for the

St. Louis *Post Dispatch* and his wife, Mary Grant, a former correspondent for the McGraw-Hill World News, to stay with them at their home in Dooneen, Ireland.

The Grants caught my attention when I read their book *White Goats and Black Bees*, a wonderfully written narrative about leaving New York City to carve out a self-sufficient life in the extremely remote, wind-blown landscape of Dooneen. During the course of our correspondence, I'd given the Grants a very loose arrival schedule, feeling, to some degree, uncomfortable because I would be hitchhiking from Shannon to Bantry. They were exceptionally generous in response. Donald had scribbled in the letter I carried on me, "Then, we will see you when we see you."

I had calculated the distance between Shannon and Bantry was less than 120 miles maximum or two days of hitchhiking—tops. I had not considered being sidetracked by two days of water-skiing on the Shannon River with one of Ireland's most famous tenors and his wife, traveling with tinkers, being stuck in torrential rains and being forced to sleep on church pews, renting a motorcycle and changing trajectory altogether, entering a dart tournament in the small town of Balleydehob, and spending two days on the Great Blasket Islands during a horrific storm with a woman who was illegally living on the island. Then there was Gabe, publican of Gabe's Pub. How could I possibly have imagined or envisioned any of this?

It was, after all, an isle of banshees and tricksters.

The Great Blasket Islands

One of the books I carried with me to Ireland was an Oxford University Press collectible titled *Twenty Years A-Growing*, by Maurice O'Sullivan. In his first-person account of his childhood life on the Great Blasket Island, O'Sullivan proved to be an engaging and remarkable storyteller, weaving stories from folktales passed down from family members at the firesides of many a cold and wet winter night.

The preface of the book made me think back across my life to my grandmother Rosy, when she would spin her tales at Sunday supper. O'Sullivan wrote, "It was a tender thought that struck me to write this book for the entertainment and laughter of the old women of the Blasket Island, who showed me great love and affection when I used to call on them during the long winter nights." I can't speak for my brother or sister, but in the telling of my grandmother's stories, I often felt drunk by the end of the night, as though the banshees and silkies were just barely out of reach. And, I suspected, just as I imagined the flavor of O'Sullivan's narratives morphed, so did my grandmother's tales as they were embellished and enriched by the telling and retelling.

The coastal seascape of County Kerry is harshly cut by the elements: scrabble hard and bare, clawed pastures, windswept, jagged, and relentlessly exposed to a constant discord of howling wind and rain. It is a brooding, rugged landscape haunted by thick, dark, rumbling clouds and held ransom by the treacherous currents of the Atlantic Ocean.

When I left the Grants' home, I carried a slip of paper with the name of a man who might know of a man who might take me across to the Blasket Islands. I was properly forewarned by them that, although it had not been their experience and they did not actually know the man in question, it was rumored that he was prone to "the heavy drink." The Grants were not the sort of couple who offered such commentary lightly. However, given the fact that I had been in Ireland for close to a month and had rarely entered an evening's folly that wasn't punctuated with several characters prone to "the heavy drink"—myself among the best of them—the warning seemed altogether overly protective. I paid little heed to their words of caution.

It was midafternoon when I found Sean, along with his brother Johnnie, who agreed to take me over to the island the following morning but only if the weather was good. I was to meet them at the dock where we would take their wicker-framed, tar-covered canvas currah across open water to the island. On the way, they would drop off their lobster pots in hopes of a "bit of a catch."

"We normally use the power skiff, but it's fallen into difficulty so we'll have to row over."

"It's fine by me," I replied.

We agreed they would drop me off on the Great Blasket early so I could walk the length and I was to meet them by four p.m. or "thereabouts" and we'd return to the mainland. If the weather became too treacherous to cross to the island, they'd leave me there and return the following day to pick me up.

"And if it's inclement weather the second day?" I asked.

"The very same," replied Johnnie nonchalantly.

"I would have to stay overnight on the island?"

"Or, you could swim back," laughed Sean, "but I wouldn't recommend it."

I was concerned. It wasn't that I didn't feel comfortable in any wilderness situation. I believed I could handle just about anything connected to the outdoors, but I wasn't prepared the way I would like to be. I'd already given half the agreed amount of money and there was a certain stubbornness born into me that didn't allow for me to cancel the trip, so I agreed. We shook hands.

For a reasonable fee, I found a boathouse that allowed me to store my motorcycle for the day. I purchased some supplies for the campaign to Blasket Island: two small, smoked mackerel the fish monger wrapped in a waxy brown paper, a loaf of soda bread wrapped in newspaper, a chunk of sharp cheese, a chocolate bar, a box of tea, bottled water, some McVitie digestive biscuits, and a small jar of marmalade preserves. Among the items I'd carried to Ireland was a small, white-gas Svea stove, a Swiss Army knife, a fork and spoon, and a World War II coffee mug—one that could be placed directly over the stove and double for a bowl when the need presented itself.

That evening, as I took a hearty evening meal of Guinness pie with drink and in conversation with the proprietress, Peg, I found she had a room I could rent for the night. I explained my plans for the following day and she agreed to let me leave my belongings at her home while I traveled to the island.

"And who might be taking you across?" she asked, almost as an afterthought.

"Sean and Johnnie," I replied. "They came recommended."

"You don't say now," she replied. There was a slight hesitance in her voice.

"Should I be concerned?" I asked her. "Are they not dependable?"

"You do know that nobody lives on the island anymore, don't you? Haven't since '53." She had avoided my question.

"I do. That's why I'm interested in going. To see what it might have been like."

"I've never understood it myself," she replied without judgment. "What's done is done."

"Well, I hope it's not a mistake."

"And so do I," she said. I would realize later she'd not weighed in on my question about the brothers.

During the night, a loud explosion that shook the small room awakened me. I jolted upright in bed and listened to the night erupt in storm. Clashes of thunder split the sky and lightning and rain pounded relentlessly on the window with such violence that at times I felt the window would be pummeled in. With each crack of lightning, my room would illuminate in the most ghoulish forms. If the night continued into the morning as such, the trip would be called off and, I suspected, I would lose my deposit. There was nothing I could do, so I burrowed back under the thick quilt and quickly fell into a deep sleep.

I awoke to a room bathed in brilliant morning light. When I pulled back the laced curtains and peered out, I was taken by Irish light, crystal clarity of breathtaking beauty, that split second in the final focus of a camera lens that brings everything into exactness before the shutter clicks.

Thirty-four years later and I still remember the vividness of this small coastal town coming to life in such a manner that it has been locked into my memory like a river's tooth.

I quickly packed, deposited my gear with Peg, and made off to the pier where I'd agreed to meet Sean and Johnnie. They were already at the pier stacking lobster pots into the currah. I dropped my kit and offered to give them a hand.

"It'll be a fine day for a crossing," offered Sean.

"It certainly looks that way," I replied, feeling much more comfortable about putting in with the brothers. I could see the island across the bay and I was excited to get onto the morning. The bay was smooth and silky, with the tide beginning to drop. The surrounding rocks were laden with mussels, and thick seaweed undulated in the ebb and flow in a fluid and hypnotic dance.

Very little conversation took place on the journey. With little wasted motion, Johnnie sitting in the stern of the currah, baited and dropped the lobster traps overboard while Sean rowed. This was the work of brothers who'd performed this ritual their entire lives.

The currah was surprisingly light on the water and reminded me, in many ways, of the wooden dories used in Montana and Idaho from which I later often fly-fished—with the exception of two important structural designs. The currah was far lighter than its western counterpart and with its curved bottom, as opposed to a flat-bottom dory, it was also a much easier boat to manipulate on the water.

The men dropped me off at the old landing slip harbor that was not much more than a little cut through breakwater, with a promise to return at four p.m.

"Gauge your time well and enjoy."

"Thank you. I'll see you this afternoon."

"Weather and God willing."

As their blades cut into the water, a bit of panic set in. The thought crossed my mind that if anything happened to Sean and Johnnie, I'd be left on the island alone. True, I had a couple of days' worth of food and Peg knew where I was going, so ultimately, a rescue party would be sent out, but much could go wrong in a hurry on such a remote island.

For the next several hours, I walked the island, climbing first to the highest point to survey the remaining islands of the Blasket archipelago. The Great Blasket itself teemed with rabbit, presumably brought to the island as a food source only later to become feral, or perhaps released by the last inhabitants to be removed from the island in 1953 by the British. This conjecture appealed to me most, a final gesture from an oppressed population in a circumstance of overwhelming power. It would be so Irish.

To be certain, it is a tough landscape, but there is surprising color in the yellow-flowered gorse bushes and moorland purple heather, hearty scrabble plants, steadfast against the blowing winds. The bird life distracted me greatly, and since I was an amateur birder I found myself making entries into my journal and noting the abundant bird life: kittiwakes, puffins, petrels, razorbills, and guillemots. Since these were not my backyard birds, it was quite a pleasurable discovery.

What I hadn't noticed was a buildup of dark clouds to the northwest closing in toward the archipelago at an alarming rate.

I was at the very northern end of the island and decided I'd best scramble back to the southeast where I hadn't yet done any exploring. My original plan was to head to the outlying reaches of the island first and then return to the southeast and spend a couple of hours looking at the remains of the village until Sean and Johnnie arrived to collect me. I had not taken into consideration the mercurial and bipolar landscape with its dramatic and ruthless mood swings.

In the beginning the wind offered a warning with short powerful gusts and then began a steady, deep-throated howling. The rain, on a slant, was light at first and then harder and more forceful until it lashed at me, stinging my face. I had to shield my face with my arm and squint to see. In no time, collar of my jacket pulled up to my face, tweed cap pulled down over my ears, I started to get drenched. I was exposed, completely exposed to the capricious nature of the storm. My vision was limited to a few feet in front of me and I was afraid I would become lost but more concerned that I might become hypothermic. If I could somehow make my way to the old village I might be able to seek refuge in the corner of an abandoned house. Perhaps I could find a scrap or two of wood, a broken chair, a plank from a table, anything at all, and build a spit of fire. I'd cling to the notion.

I stayed as close to the ridgeline as I felt comfortable in doing. Because I knew the island ran north and south, my plan was to head south and even if I was off a few degrees, I still had a chance of stumbling onto the cove. There was only one sandy beach on the island, and from there I was fairly certain I could find the abandoned village.

An hour later, truly and utterly drenched to the bones and with no signs of the storm letting up, I looked at my watch and realized there was no possibility Sean and Johnnie would be able to retrieve me. I could not fault them. I was starting to chill and my teeth began to chatter. Worst of all, I was losing hope. The prospect of staying the night on the island was not only frightening, it was dangerous and potentially life-threatening.

Think man, think!

I unslung my rucksack and placed it on the ground. Kneeling down in the wet, I bent over the sack to keep as much rain out as possible. I undid the clasp, plunged my hands inside, and fumbled about until I could feel the mackerel wrapped in its waxy paper. I strapped the clasp shut again and tucked the mackerel inside my jacket where I was able to slide a crossed string to the side of the wrapping and reveal the head of one of the mackerels. I bit through the mackerel's head and held it in my mouth, sucking on the oil and salt.

Had a single soul come upon me at that moment, they would have seen a bent and broken young man, wild-eyed and frightened, cradled protectively over something they would not recognize as a rucksack, with a mouth full of some ungodly flesh dripping from the side of his beard. What they could not possibly know or understand was that this single act offered more than sustenance; it offered the possibility of life. It granted a foolish young vagabond a moment to consider history, to call upon his own instincts and ancestors for survival. It offered him hope that somehow he might claw his way to another day.

Whatever respite the mackerel offered me in terms of confidence was soon dashed by the deepening storm. The rain slashed at the island and it was apparent that if I didn't find some shelter, I would most probably not make it through the night. The temperature was dropping rapidly and I had no real sense how far I was from the village.

I began to shiver so I picked up the pace in an effort to get my body thermostat cranked up. My wool sweater had served me well to date but was now hopelessly wet. My jacket was drenched, but the danger was from the inside where it was impossible to keep rain from running down my neck. I cursed the fact that I'd left a Sierra Design, full-body poncho back at Peg's. Although it wasn't completely waterproof, it had a hood that would have kept the water from saturating me. I thought of Jack London's short story "To Build a Fire," and how the simple act of letting your hands get too cold to light matches in the wild Yukon had cost the protagonist his life. It is the smallest things that begin chain reactions. The poncho weighed nothing and I left it behind because the weather looked good. It was so dangerously amateurish and, worse, I knew better.

I stumbled against the storm and kept to what I hoped would be a direct route to the tiny village of Gob and the harbor. If I hit White Strand, the only stretch of beach on the rocky island, I knew I could find the village. And there, perhaps, some shelter. I hummed "Foggy Dew" and placed foot in front of foot, head tucked and bent into my own fear.

Peat. A whiff. Distinctive and oily. Perfumed. Making no sense at all. Here on a forgotten island. Cruel, it seemed. Hallucinations. Vapor ghosts on a desert highway, appearing and disappearing. Just enough to make me think of a roaring fire? The night swallowed light, and began to swallow me. It made it hard not to cry. Is it time? In what sense? Such a bad, bad movie. "Plug on man . . . plug on!" And I did. A half hour, perhaps an hour. I ceased humming and moved beyond the warmth my humming had to offer.

Turf. Turf. Turf. Turf on the island? None of this made any sense. A small light flickered in what seemed to be a small hut.

Turf, thick as tobacco now. A low building, a house, home, a dream. It could be a trap. *From what? Metcalf, from what?* Ask good questions. I'm babbling to myself. *Banshees. Witches,*

I mumble. *A silkie, for Christ's sake!* Preposterous? My grandmother was not lying. But this was a trap. I was convinced of it. *I must go slowly. I must be careful. I must be sure.* My knock at the door was soft.

"Holy Mary Mother of God! Come in now, come in."

I managed to slur a few words before she reacted. "I hope I didn't startle . . ."

"Take your wet clothes off quickly." She turned her back and stoked the turf and furze-wood fire, adding an extra clump of scrap wood.

I struggled with the simple task of removing my jacket. Immediately she came to my side.

"Here now, let me give a pull," and quickly stripped me of my wet clothes, wrapping a wool shawl around me.

"I can't take your shawl from . . ."

"Stop now."

She twisted my clothes into knots, wringing as much water from them as she could. Then she strung them out on odd nails and pegs on the rafters and above the hearth to dry. From a plastic five-gallon jug she filled a teapot and placed it near the peat. Over her shoulder she beckoned me.

"Come. Get warm. Sit." She patted a three-legged stool. I shuffled over and sat. She moved to a small makeshift table and grabbed a small pint bottle. Twisting off the cap, she extended the bottle. "This will warm you."

"Thank you."

"You are welcome." She disappeared into an adjacent room. I quickly studied the interior. A small, built-in cupboard, stripped of anything burnable, held some kitchen utensils, cook kit, odds and ends, including candles and strikes. Some wicker lobster pots stacked inside, which I thought odd. A slightly listing kitchen table, propped up as best as could be done, a small bench, a work table of sorts with balls of wool, needles, and some handmade stocking caps. In the corner, a cot folded in on itself and tied securely with rope.

Still, I was shivering uncontrollably and the world was lop-sided indeed. She returned in seconds and pushed an under-shirt of sorts into my hands, a pair of dungarees and a cable-knit sweater. I fumbled with the shirt.

"Here," she said, taking the shirt from my lap. "Hands up over your head."

I obeyed like a small and frightened child, uncertain and suspicious. And the thought crossed my mind that she was, or perhaps could be, a silkie. This place, the cold and bitterly harsh brutish landscape would be the perfect refuge from the underworld and the overworld; a staging spot, so to speak, where a silkie might envisage what price such a Faustian bargain might extract. Who was to say? I looked carefully for an epidermis, a pelt. Would that be fair to call it a pelt? Another mammal's body? I swear I could smell salt on her but not exactly. Closer, possibly the ocean? Next, she helped me into the thick, cable-knit sweater and the deep rich smell of lanolin on the wool offered me a raft of hope. It was the smell of warmth.

It was odd, the sleeves, that is, they were only three-quarter length, as though the knitter had run out of wool and simply stopped.

"It's my husband's," she said, noticing my curiosity. "He's a fisherman—lobsters," she offered, as if I would know. When I didn't reply, she added, "Knitted such as to keep the sweater out of the water."

"Of course." I was nervous. Here I was in another man's clothes on the Great Blasket Island, on a dangerous night. How might that play out should he arrive at any moment? What could a man think?

"Do you," hesitantly and carefully, "live here?"

"No. It's against the law." For the first time, she looked uncomfortable. "Why?"

"I don't know," I mumbled awkwardly. "It just seems cozy, comfortable, lived in, that's all." These were not the words I meant to say because we both knew I was lying, trying to backpedal. At best, it was a halfway station, a place between worlds.

"When I opened the door," she said quietly, "I thought you might be him."

"I apologize. . . . I startled you. I'm very sorry."

"No," she replied, "you were in need."

"Thank you."

Silence held thick. She took a loaf of Irish soda bread and cut off two dense slices, spreading them with butter and layering them with thick slabs of sharp cheese. Then a cup of tea.

Slowly I began to warm up. Thunderclaps exploded outside and the storm deepened. In my mind a series of questions began to collect. Light from the candles danced against the walls. I wondered, perhaps, if she wasn't a gypsy or she and her husband were squatting on the island against the law. Or, fugitives from the law. Or, illegally dropping lobster pots around Blasket, or worse yet, stealing other lobster pots. Or, in fact, did she truly have a husband?

There was too much in the way of provisions for this to be a casual campaign around the island. More dangerous for me, her husband's whereabouts. The same sense of mystery, I suspected, could be asked of me. A half-drowned Yank on the brink of hypothermia in the pitch of a storm, appears from darkness and raps on a hideaway door. Strange, to be certain, but still, she opened the door. I did not know her name.

"My name is Jeff," I finally said as I stood up and offered out my hand. "Thank you."

"And mine is Clare," she replied, taking my hand firmly in hers. "You're not from here about, are you?" She laughed and so did I.

"No," I answered, completely disarmed by her wide smile, adding, "I bet it's easy to spot the tourists on the island."

Clare laughed and the tension and urgency of the night dissolved around us.

"Glory be to God," she exclaimed. "What, if I might ask, brought you to this forsaken island?"

"Stories by my grandmother. And you?"

"My husband," she answered quietly. "I'm waiting for my husband."

"My God, he's not out in this weather, is he?"

I was truly alarmed for Clare. I could only imagine what it might be like on such a night in a small currah battling against the choppy and swelling sea. Anywhere out in the Great Sound would be treacherous. Deadly.

The math of this possibility did not add up; regardless, I suspected how good a boatman he might be. He would be a man who knew what to do. Unlike me and the surprise of events, he would be a fisherman who knew how to survive. I surmised that he must have tucked into some cove, a tiny spit of beach on one of the other islands, and doing so, would overturn his currah and find safety under the ribbed framework of the boat.

"How long has he been gone?" I asked, trying to stay calm.

"Over two weeks now," Clare answered, looking straight and deep into my eyes.

And because I said nothing, in fact did not know what to say against the implications, she breathed, "He went under, my husband, Liam. He went out and got caught and nobody has seen him since. I won't leave the island until I recover his body," she said, as resolute as I ever heard. With that, she blew out the candles and wished me a good night's sleep.

Gabe's Pub

It was a windswept and balmy midafternoon when I arrived in the small village of Ballydehob. I'd punched through terribly foul weather on my motorcycle and was damp and bone cold. Even in a thick wool sweater, oil-clothed outer jacket, thermal underwear, and rubberized foul weather bibs, I'd chilled. I took a small room in a B&B, paid the proprietress in advance, shed my clothes, spread out my kit to dry, and took a long deep, luxuriating hot bath with Dr. Bronner's peppermint liquid soap.

After a much-needed nap, I wandered into town to take a pint of local beer, grab a bite, and get a full night's rest before meeting Donald and Mary Grant. To some small degree I felt guilty that I had not arrived in Dooneen on the date I'd promised the Grants. They'd been kind enough to invite me to stay with them in their cottage and I had returned this kindness by disappearing into the seam of Ireland. I couldn't exactly explain what had happened to me, because I didn't understand it myself. It never occurred to me that the Grants wouldn't completely understand since they themselves had come under the spell of Ireland. When I was finally able to ring Mary on the phone and apologize for my lack of manners, she laughed, "Jeff, we will see you when you arrive. We're not going anywhere. Travel safely."

That was that.

Finding a pub in Ballydehob was more difficult than one might expect. Not for the obvious reason, because there were few pubs, but just the opposite. Ballydehob had more pubs than a person could shake a stick at! Per capita, I can only think of one other place that had as many bars and that would be Stanley, Idaho, in the Sawtooth Mountains, which hosted three bars for thirty-nine people. Ballydehob would be a close second.

For no other reason than the fact that I liked the painting above Gabe's pub, I elected to stop at this establishment for my evening meal. The pub's sign was squished between two white windows above the main floor of the pub. Laced white linens covered the windows which I presumed offered a bit of privacy to the occupants of Gabe's. In the painting, two men stood at the forefront of several casks of beer. They were dressed in dark trousers with white shirts, sleeves rolled up and snappy-patterned red vests. Both men wore dark fedora hats. One man appeared to be making a toast to his friend—his friend carrying a full keg of beer on his shoulder heading into a pub. It would be, I suspected, Murphy's Irish Stout.

I couldn't have made a better selection. Gabe's was full of the Irish. Men of all ages were having pints and carrying on with the language of any bar. It was an eavesdropping Mecca. I overheard a scholarly dissertation on the reason Guinness Stout tasted different in America than it did in Ireland and immediately followed that with a heated commentary on the best horses to race along the Irish coastline. The room was hazed in a layer of pipe tobacco and cigarette smoke. Bartenders at the back bar were drawing beer at breakneck speed and the servers carried trays through the crowd without spilling a drop. Two young men played live music and occasionally laughter would spill up over the music.

I sat at the bar and when the barkeep came to take my order, I asked for his recommendation. He looked me over, turned away, grabbed a pint glass and filled it with a Murphy's Irish Stout, scraped the foam, and placed it in front of me. "Murphy's," he said. "The first one is on Gabe's." I thanked him and before I could add anything else, he offered his hand. "And I'm Gabe." I introduced myself to him, gave him a brief history of why I had come to Bal-lydehob, and then proceeded to ask him if he knew the Grants. "In a fashion, I do," he replied in a thick Cork accent. "They're the Yanks that bought in Dooneen?" He paused before adding, "'Tis a bit strange to me. Leaving the states to move here. Isn't it?"

He introduced me to a couple sitting alongside me. Korin and Declan who hailed from the UK and were, in fact, looking to purchase country property, so the idea did not seem so far-fetched to them.

"So," I asked, "is the pub always this full?"

"Tonight's Gabe's annual dart tournament," Korin answered, adding with a wink, "and that's pretty important around here."

Gabe rang a bar bell and the selections for the tournament were posted and bracketed. After studying the pairings, somebody hollered that Old Thomas was without a partner. Gabe did a quick survey of the pub to see if he could find a fill-in and when he couldn't, he bee-lined over to us. "Declan, could you do us a favor and stand in?" When Declan admitted he'd never played in his life, Gabe was surprised.

"Never? Not once in your life?"

"Never. I can't say as I have," offered Declan apologetically.

"Jeff, what about you? Are you a dart man?"

"No, but if you're in a pinch, I'd give it a whirl," I replied, feel-ing relatively certain he'd be able to find a substitute.

"Great," Gabe said, "Come now, and let me introduce you to Old Thomas."

To this day, some thirty-five years later, I am still uncertain if Old Thomas had any idea how we ended up becoming dart part-ners. Old Thomas was perhaps in his early eighties, with failing eyesight and a significant hearing loss. Worse than that, he was paired up with a complete novice, a Yank to boot, who had never once thrown a dart. Grossly unfair.

Round after round of darts and stout, Old Thomas and I managed to scrape by win after win. It turned out, at least in that moment, in that window, I could throw darts and Old Thomas had not lost the touch in any fashion.

The darts lay deeply imbedded in his genetic code. With the crowd clearly on our side and pints being sent over to our standing table, old Thomas and I won the tournament. We hugged each other and the crowd sort of lifted us up in the air.

Then, we put on "the craic" until half-ten where, by the laws enforced by the UK at the time, pubs were required to close up but not before pledging their allegiance to the Queen.

I did not want the evening to stop and I told Gabe so. "Stay close to Korin and Declan. We are not done by any means." While Gabe and his lovely wife, Michelle, closed Gabe's and said good-night to all, half of us walked around back where we were greeted and invited back in to continue the celebration. By locking the front door, Gabe had, in a pretzel logic way, fulfilled his legal responsibilities.

When we were brought back into the pub, he explained that the cash register had been closed out so, if we'd like to offer a "gratuity" it would be appreciated. Gabe simply placed a milk pail on the bar counter and for the next two hours of drinking, people were on the honor system to pay what they owed and it worked.

Korin, Declan, and Gabe wondered if I could stay through the week to witness the sailing race from Cowes, UK, around Fastnet Lighthouse and back, a trip of almost seven hundred miles.

"With a great camera, one can get some smashing photographs of sailboats with full spinnakers unfurled," Gabe said with great enthusiasm. "We're planning to take a boat out from Baltimore to get a closer view."

When I discovered Gabe didn't have a camera, I offered him the use of my Minolta with a telephoto lens.

It was a plan without solid legs.

The camera was expensive and would virtually end any recorded images of the remainder of my travels in Ireland. Gabe steadfastly refused, pointing out that we'd all had a bit to drink, suggesting perhaps I'd not carefully considered what I was doing. But I insisted. If Gabe would promise to mail the camera to me in the states, it was his. End of the story and Gabe finally acquiesced and reluctantly took the camera.

As much as I wished to stay in Ballydehob, I simply couldn't. I was expected by the Grants and it would be bad form to delay the visit again. The early morning ended with Gabe insisting that I take the dart trophy back to the states with me. I explained I couldn't do so because I was on a motorcycle, but promised that I would return within five years to defend my title. He shook my hand and then pulled me into a huge bear hug.

"Ah, Jeff, that would be a great thing if you did. Not many people return back to Ballydehob. It's a bit out of the way, isn't it?"

"Perhaps," I replied. "But a promise made is a debt unpaid."

"I like that," he smiled.

"Robert Service," I answered, "The Cremation of Sam McGee," and then crossed the cobblestone road and headed to my B&B for a few hours of much-needed sleep before meeting the Grants.

Finally, the Grants

Seven hours following the dart tournament, I was packed and ready to head off to Dooneen to meet Donald and Mary Grant.

At the breakfast table in the B&B, I polished off several pieces of soda bread slathered in butter, eggs, tomatoes, sausage, some boiled potatoes, and a couple of pots of tea. It helped but I was still wounded from putting on the "craic" the night before.

Slowly I began to piece together the previous night; the meeting of Korin and Declan, Gabe and Michelle, Nash, the Coughlans, Old Thomas, the dart tournament and a cast of others whose names and faces bled together in a ruddy-faced snapshot of all my relatives growing up in New York.

My grandmother would have loved every liquid breath of the story.

Then, I thought of the camera.

The camera might have been a mistake. Understanding that in the tilted moment of the previous night it might have made perfect sense. But this morning, the idea of having offered up my new Minolta 35mm camera and a sliding telephoto lens to a perfect (although through a series of marginally tipsy declarations of brotherhood) stranger didn't pencil out. Still, I thought, I might be able to get it back. I could drop by the pub with the intention of bidding farewell to Gabe and Michelle. When the topic of the camera arose and Gabe offered to give it back, I could look genuinely disappointed. Both of us might save face and we could both offer the most genuine of compliments to each other. It might have worked except for the simple fact that Gabe's was closed and the streets were deserted.

With no other brilliant idea, I pushed off toward Dooneen.

I had a vague sense of the direction to the Grants' home. Donald's letter with directions now seemed very vague. I was to head toward Dunmanus Bay, which Donald had written they could see from their window. "If you can see the castle, you are close. The lanes will get smaller and you'll have to look to find our place. It's tucked back behind the hedges."

For most of the trip I hardly saw another person. Occasionally the odd farmer might offer a nod or not. The landscape from Ballydehob southwest toward Mizen Head became more exposed and rugged. For much of the morning I was certain that I was headed in the wrong direction. Intuitively, I knew that couldn't be the case, but it was hard to reconcile how these two New Yorkers would move from the excitement of Manhattan and high-profile journalistic jobs to the backwaters of southern Ireland. It just didn't register.

I started to run out of road and the lanes began to narrow; I pulled the motorcycle to the side of the lane and revisited Donald's letter. Before withdrawing the letter from my rucksack, I sat atop a beautiful stone wall, impressively set without mortar, and, after several attempts against the wind, I managed to light my pipe.

The wind was relentless and my face, reddened by the elements, felt raw. It occurred to me that if I climbed off the wall, and dropped to the ground, I could lean up against the wall, be removed from the wind, and glean some warmth from the sun. I set my pipe on a stone slab, turned the collar up on my jacket, tucked my chin down, and fell asleep. It didn't take long.

When I jerked myself awake, I was surprised to find a black and white Australian sheep dog, sitting directly in front of me as though I had been herded to the wall.

Coming up the road was a young man. I stood up, dusted myself off, and greeted him.

"You've got a beautiful dog," I offered as an icebreaker.

"Thank you! Come." The dog moved and sat to his side.

"My name's Jeff," I said, extending my hand out.

"Jerry," he said, offering his in return. "Looking for the Grants, are you?"

"Yes," I replied. "I'm trying to find their home."

Jerry started to laugh. I got that uncomfortable feeling that one gets when they are outside of a joke. I laughed myself.

"Just come from their home myself. They're expecting you."

"So, it's not that far?"

"Behind you is their property. Go down the lane to the gate and that's their home."

He was kind enough not to laugh. I was perhaps only six hundred yards from the house.

I thanked him, shook his hand again, and puttered down the road to the Grants' front gate. I walked to the front door, knocked, and waited. Donald Grant opened up the door and greeted me. He was taller than I anticipated, slender and straight-backed, and reminded me a bit of Gary Cooper.

He was not at all what I'd expected. He looked like he belonged. Donald called to his wife, Mary, who came to the door. She was wiping her hands on a kitchen towel.

"Come in, please. I just took some soda bread out of the oven and we were going to have it with homemade goat cheese and tea."

"Thank you," I replied, and stepped across the threshold into their home.

I spent the next four days with the Grants following them through their daily routine. The morning began with dark coffee or tea, a thick slice of soda bread slathered in butter and topped with goat cheese and fresh herbs.

Following breakfast I would head off with Donald and we would work on the property or head down to the bay and set crab pots. It seemed a perfect life to a young and restless man like myself.

This sense of self-sufficiency resonated with me on many levels, but I came to realize just how much work it took to make this look idyllic. The Grants confided how they'd been overwhelmed by the demands of such a simple life. It was a full-time job making ends meet and they were adamant about letting guests and friends know that this sort of existence was not for everybody.

On my final day, I excused myself for a hike. I told Donald and Mary I wanted to take a last walk around the area before leaving. Instead, I headed to a section on the upper end of the property where a rock wall had fallen over and was in need of repair. During summer months when school let out, I worked construction and was a fairly competent stone mason. The walls were dry stacked, stone upon stone like a giant jigsaw puzzle held together without mortar. It took me close to four hours of hard work before it was completely finished. When I'd completed the wall I returned to the Grants for a final dinner of crab, a garden salad, bread, cheese, and some beer. I said nothing about mending the wall. It would be a surprise.

Before turning in for the night, I thanked Donald and Mary for their gracious hospitality and promised that, if I could, I'd try to visit them again. I truly had no idea if that would happen but I certainly hoped it would. In the first morning light, I made a couple of sandwiches, wrote them a note, and placed my remaining pipe tobacco in a small paper bag for Donald. I stepped outside into the damp cold of Ballydehob, fired up the motorcycle, and headed north to Dublin.

Driving Lesson

To this day I am still uncertain why the idea seemed to make sense, or, perhaps more surprisingly, that my girlfriend, Alana—now my wife of thirty years—agreed to such an outlandish proposal, but she did.

We were living in Oxford, England, on the second floor of an old manor home called Tubney Warren. I was on sabbatical from my school for a year to pursue a liberal course of study in the humanities. Before departing the states, in what was a decidedly risky move, I'd invited Alana to quit her job, sell whatever she could, and join me in any adventures that might unfold during the course of the year. We hadn't been dating each other for very long but there was some powerful magic indeed. In retrospect, it wasn't much of a proposal and it surprised me when she agreed. Given the chance again, I think she would still do the same. There is adventure in her bones.

Three months after purchasing a beat-up Renault sedan from a local mechanic in Oxford, Alana still felt uncomfortable driving on the opposite side of the road. In August, we'd purchased Raleigh ten-speed bicycles fitted with front and side baskets to handle our daily undertakings. As fall weather began to turn nasty, there were times when driving a car was an unavoidable necessity.

I'd been running a poker clinic—populated by students from Corpus Christi College—to make a bit of extra cash, and for the month of October we'd planned on taking the profits and heading off on a campaign that would take us from England to Ireland and eventually Scotland, following whatever path inspired us. Our itinerary would be informed by literature and landscape and we agreed to keep ourselves open to any possibility. We have always traveled this way and it serves our personalities well.

Traveling off season has always held great appeal to us for many reasons. Time seems to move slower and somehow the universe opens up in a different and unassuming way. When a farmer selling goat cheese on the side of the road invites you for supper, it is easy to make time for such a gift. A postmaster and salmon boat captain in the Applecross Peninsula in the Isle of Skye took us in when a horrific coastal storm made it too dangerous to drive. It was almost ten p.m. when we banged on his door hoping to find some sort of lodging. The town had buttoned up for the season and we were getting desperate. Even if we could just pull off into his field, we could wrap ourselves up in our second-hand woolen surplus jackets and make it through the night. Above the door, a small brass plaque was inscribed with the word "Rivendell." Anybody who knew anything about the land of the Hobbits knew that Rivendell was one of the most remote outposts of elves in J. R. R. Tolkien's fictional Middle Earth landscape. This was a wild card and most certainly worth a try.

After banging on the large brass doorknocker, I had serious misgivings about the plan. We were in the thick of a squall and the rain was pounding with relentless force. It was too late to be knocking on anybody's door particularly since we were absolute strangers. How would this circumstance be received in my own city? I shuddered to think, but at the minimum it would include a baseball bat hidden behind one's back and some very unkind words.

Guardedly, the door opened and revealed a rather tall, slender man, middle-aged with an angular face, red hair, and a disarming smile given the particular state of affairs. "Yes?" he said, a strange greeting for such horrific conditions and at such an odd hour.

I raised my eyes to the plaque above the threshold and said, "Gandalf sent us."

For a moment he just stared at us, and then he laughed and greeted us both as though we were long lost friends and quickly invited us out of the storm and into his home. We joined his family at the hearth and they quickly prepared a fresh salmon dinner for us. Around the fire, Alana braided his daughter's hair while our host and I swapped stories about our lives in rapid succession. That night was as cozy as any I can remember. It was thick with laughter and terrific single-malt Scotch. To be offered shelter and a succulent, home-cooked meal at eleven o'clock at night under such nightmarish weather conditions was beyond anything either of us had ever experienced. To this day, that chance encounter has never been equaled. Such was the generosity and hospitality we experienced all throughout the one-month adventure driving the back roads of Ireland and Scotland.

After a few days in Dublin, we headed due south to revisit some wonderful people I had met five years earlier when I traveled across Ireland on a motorcycle. I'd built these stories up with such warmth and light that I felt, guiltily so, they would never match up to those imagined in Alana's mind.

As we moved toward Northern Ireland, the landscape and political climate changed dramatically. This was to be expected, but we hadn't prepared ourselves completely for what we would soon see or experience. On the far side of history, 1982 had been a violent year. On the twentieth of July, some five months prior to this adventure, I'd been staying in a bed and breakfast not far from Hyde Park when a terrorist bomb exploded and killed seven of the Queen's parade horses. The Provisional Irish Republican Army immediately took credit for the deaths of civilians, horses and eleven of Her Majesty's soldiers.

I'd been jogging in Hyde Park earlier that morning only hours before the explosion. I'd showered and headed off to tour a few of my favorite museums when the horror of that day began appearing on televisions in storefront windows.

Panic gripped the city and the psychological terror of the act was smothering. Upon returning to my hotel, I saw that the windows had been shattered by the blast. The manager seemed truly relieved to discover I had not been one of the innocent tourists wounded or killed in the bombing. I was allowed to collect my belongings and was relocated to another small boutique hotel. I'm not a jogger. In fact, I can't think of any form of exercise I dislike more than jogging. But on that day, jogging, quite literally, saved my life.

As the two of us continued north on our journey, the laughter and light seemed to give way to suspicion and darkness. The landscape appeared more foreign and the Irish we encountered were less friendly and hospitable. We tried to moderate our paranoia, but subtle discriminations were becoming undeniably pointed. Stopping for supper at a busy pub in Quinn, Ireland, we were informed there was neither food nor drink for our kind. All the while, the second publican at the bar was pulling drafts and the servers were bringing out food to waiting tables.

"Why would that be?" I asked politely.

"Because we don't serve your kind." The barkeep's eyes betrayed no sign of regret in his statement. We left the pub and crossed the street to the Renault.

"They think we're English," Alana said. "Our license plates. The car is registered in England."

"I suppose you're right," I replied, feeling a sense of loss and reduction in such foolish suppositions. Clearly, we were being watched.

"Maybe this wasn't such a good idea," she said, adding, "the farther north we go, the less life there is. You look at the teenagers and there is no happiness in them. They look old."

It was the truth. We were entering into a war zone the farther north we traveled. The concern was that we might actually be pushing the boundary of good fortune, but in the end, we both felt we needed to see Belfast so we could attempt to comprehend and digest, in any manner or form, how deep the politics of history and religion clashed. Trying to spin the moment, I offered Alana a thought.

"This would be a perfect time to teach you to drive on the other side of the road, huh?"

"Are you crazy? Here?"

"It's the perfect spot. We haven't run into any traffic and I can guarantee you we won't run into any tourists."

We paralleled the west side of Lough Neagh with the idea of dropping down on Newtownabbey into Holywood and then Belfast. Alana was proving to be a calm and careful driver.

Taking time for lunch at a small local pub north of the lake, we then headed toward Holywood. It was mid-afternoon and clouds were darkening. Snow mixed with sleet and the Renault's heater was marginal at best. Rounding a corner just outside of a small village, Alana suddenly came on a roadblock. Two English soldiers, well armed with automatic weapons and relatively protected by a sandbag wall, held their hands up for our vehicle to stop. In a moment of panic, Alana hit the gas instead of the brakes. The car lurched and died ten feet beyond the guardhouse.

By the time we could recover our composure, four armed soldiers from the British Army had surrounded our vehicle with weapons leveled at our heads. We were commanded to roll down our windows slowly. As we did so, the soldier on Alana's side was swearing violently at her. Her driver's license was demanded along with insurance and registration papers for the Renault. I moved to open the glove box.

"Keep your hands where we can see them or I'll blow your fockin' head off. Who told you to move?"

"Nobody," I said cautiously, "I just thought I could help."

"If we want your help we'll bloody well ask!" Spittle landed on my jacket. I did not move to wipe it off.

Alana looked at me. I could tell she was afraid. Then, almost inaudibly, she said to me, "My license is in the trunk of the car." It was against the law to be without your license on your person when driving. This was not the time nor circumstance to try to explain. We'd run a roadblock and as far as they were concerned, we were dangerous.

"Her international driver's license is in her kit in the boot of the car. I can get it if you'd like."

"Nobody is opening the fockin' boot."

"I've got my papers, license, and everything necessary if you'd let me reach into the jockey box."

"Go on then! Move slowly." He'd placed the gun close to the side of my head as I moved toward the jockey box.

I took my gloves off slowly and produced the necessary papers and handed them over to him.

I have no filter on my own sense of humor. This was not the time to laugh under any circumstance, but the thought crossed my mind that if Alana and I both ducked beneath the window and I yelled "Fire!" the soldiers on each side of the car would shoot each other and the same with those at the front and rear of the Renault. I started to smile and just as quickly, Alana shot me a glance that stifled the urge.

The soldier tried two or three times to open up my driver's license without taking off his gloves.

To ease the tension, or so I thought, I commented, "We're all thumbs today, aren't we?"

"You bloody well better shut the fock up if you know what's good for you!" I did, and after they had checked my papers and asked what we were doing on the outskirts of Belfast, they passed us on.

Following the incident, once we were allowed to continue on, Alana asked me to drive. She'd had enough. I drove. We attempted to deconstruct the events of what had transpired. No matter how many ways we tried to rearrange the narrative, it was not a pretty story. It could have been worse, much worse, and although I did not speak it, my instinct was to turn back to England. But we were so close to Belfast and there was such a journalistic sense of curiosity that I felt drawn to the darkness. We agreed to push on.

Rounding a bend we came up directly behind a Royal Army armored personnel carrier. Young soldiers dressed in camouflage combat gear, regiment berets smartly tight to their heads and automatic weapons at the ready, sat facing each other in the back of the carrier. The two soldiers at the gate seemed to study us closely. They did not smile. Instead they took us in with their gaze.

The road was a double-striped non-passing zone. I eased off the gas and let some distance spread between our vehicle and the personnel carrier. Hills rolled down to the road and then flattened out in a broad sweep. I began to suggest that we might take a bed and breakfast in the next town we came upon when automatic rifle shots came cracking out of the hills in our direction.

At first it simply didn't register until Alana cried out. The personnel carrier slammed on its brakes and soldiers piled out from the interior, firing weapons as they ran for cover. Angled as such, the road was blocked.

"Fuck! Get down, Alana." I grabbed her and pulled her below window level. We were pinned behind the truck. Without thought, I slid down in the seat, keeping my head slightly above the rim of the door and slammed the Renault into gear and careened off the side of the road out into a wide field. The car slid and fishtailed but I kept my foot to the pedal putting as much distance as I possibly could between the ambush and ourselves. Behind us, we could hear the rat-tat-tatting of automatic weapons.

It took us some time to figure out how to get back onto the tarmac. When we were far enough away that I felt I could safely check the Renault, I stopped the car to see if we'd been hit by the random firefight. To our relief, we were unscathed but we worried about the earlier events of the day. Would they be looking for us following our experience at the roadblock? Might it be possible that shortly after we were given permission to carry on, an ambush had occurred on British forces? How would we have looked upon this series of events if the roles were reversed? There had been no vehicles on the road between the personnel carrier and us. Wasn't that just a bit too convenient? Too coincidental?

Our minds raced frantically in an effort to figure out the next move. Was part one of this scene the ambush and part two strategically planted PIRA land mines farther up the road? How could we know? Circumstances, as completely inconceivable as they appear some thirty years later, could have been woven into a different narrative that would have placed us in a convoluted subplot of the events. So, we waited.

Belfast was out of the question and off the table. Back on the road with darkness approaching, we determined the best move would be to board a late-night or early-morning ferry from Larne across the North Channel to Troon or Cairnryan and find safe haven in the landscape of Scotland.

What we both realized was that this deeply politicized and violent uprising was not soon to be resolved. The Irish ethnicity that I claimed proudly as an Irish-American was not welcome rhetoric in England. Because I was an American, and because my friends and classmates were courteous, they let me tell my child-hood stories of an Irish neighborhood growing up in New York. But being Irish under the thumb of British rule was an altogether different chronicle of experiences. What I spoke of lovingly and what the British were experiencing through acts of terrorism, both in Northern Ireland and on the mainland, made the two lenses impossible to focus into any sense of historical clarity. Unfortunately, in 1982 there was no foreseeable end to the British and Irish conflict. Only hope.

Seventh Son of a Seventh Son

Of course there is danger in telling a good story too many times. Five years after winning a dart tournament in the little town of Ballydehob, Ireland, I, along with my girlfriend, Alana, were driving toward a small coastal area in County Cork not far from Bantry Bay.

I'd taken an oath some five years earlier to return to Ballydehob, where I would defend my dart championship. Since nobody in the town would ever imagine I would return, I expected a hero's welcome and perhaps a couple of good days of drinking and carrying on with Gabe and his wife, Michelle. I would revisit an American couple, authors Donald and Mary Grant, whom I had the great pleasure to spend a few days with on my previous visit to Ireland.

The thought crossed my mind that the story I had been telling and retelling my girlfriend might not hold up to the hype. This, I fully realized, was a very great distance to travel on the slight possibility things might have been as I recalled. It was raining heavily and the battered Renault we'd purchased in Oxford had a defective heater, so we were constantly wiping the interior windows with the sleeves of our jumpers.

A mathematician would have looked at this endeavor through the equation of probability. Statistically speaking, what were the odds that Gabe was still the owner of the pub? That the tournament was close to the date we would arrive and that I'd remembered? That anybody would actually remember me, or worse, that the famous night when Old Thomas and the Yank defeated all comers at the dartboard did not register in the collective memory of the folks of Ballydehob? It was too late to turn back.

Once we arrived at the edge of Ballydehob, I drove straight to Gabe's Pub. Alana has always contended that pubs and restaurants are my geographical markers, that they are my homing devices. If I have been to a small pub in the outskirts of say, Radovica, Slovenia, a single time and I were to be dropped off within a two-hundred-kilometer radius, I would have little difficulty winding my way back to the establishment. This would not be so with cathedrals and museums.

We parked at the top of the hill and walked along Main Street. To our complete dismay, Gabe's Pub was closed. With the exception of a calico cat sitting at the entrance of a shop front, Ballydehob seemed vacated. We walked about the streets. The shops were closed. This was not at all how I had imagined my triumphant return.

Finally, after some discussion, I suggested that we drop in on the Grants since their home was not far away. Alana's concern was that they weren't expecting us for a couple of days and per-haps it might be a good idea to give them notice before popping in unannounced. I should have listened to Alana because we did, in fact, find them unprepared for our early visit. Their dogs greeted us as we entered the yard. Mary was in the kitchen making goat cheese. The fragrance was an intoxicating blend of heated goat milk infused with rosemary, fennel, and chives. Three balls of goat cheese wrapped in cheesecloth were already hanging from hooks over the sink.

When I announced myself to Mary, it didn't quite register. She admonished me for not calling ahead and mentioned that she and Donald were expecting dinner guests who would be staying the night. I promptly explained, although it wasn't the case, that we'd already made arrangements at a little B&B in Schull. She seemed relieved and quickly invited us in for some biscuits and tea. She sent me outdoors to find Donald who, she was certain, was out in the pasture with the goats.

What the Grants had done to the property since I had last visited was simply transformative. I remember thinking, when I first walked with them about this same property, how impossible the task had seemed. And I recalled Donald telling me that he thought the most difficult hurdle they would face was not the hard work, but being accepted into the community. This wasn't, he assured me, something that could be done easily. There was a tremendous gap between the lifestyle he and Mary had lived in New York and their retirement to the cottage in Bantry. Retirement suggested relaxation, leisure time to pursue those interests interrupted by the real world of work. This was not, by any means, that sort of retirement. The Grants had committed fully to becoming part of a small little community in southwestern Ireland, and to be unable to bridge that social divide would be disastrous.

Donald was tending the goats when I saw him and I offered up a hardy wave which he returned. He was smoking his pipe and carried in his hand a well-worn herder's staff. Although he was still very trim and straight backed, I was taken aback at how much he had aged. To be certain, he would have been in his mid- to late sixties, and even at half his age and reasonably fit, I imagined it would be difficult to keep up with his daily routine. I brought two pouches of pipe tobacco with me as a gift. The first time we met he'd enjoyed a bowlful of my tobacco and remarked on how smooth the smoke was. It was a blend I had mixed for me in Salt Lake City at my favorite tobacconist. Donald was reluctant at first and only agreed to take the tobacco if I agreed that we'd smoke a bowlful together following tea.

The Grants were gracious hosts but I sensed that since the success of Donald's book, *White Goats and Black Bees*, they had been the recipients of many unannounced American visitors who dreamed of one day making the same change in their own lives. They did, in fact, invite us to stay for supper but we declined.

Rather, I should say I declined. What was clearly evident to me was that Alana had no history or frame of reference for the Grants other than my story. What she knew, or had heard of them, was based on a series of stories I had told her all edited and run together as a single newsreel. In the narrative, adventure led to adventure and although my first visit riding a motorcycle across the length of Ireland was one of the richest and profoundly impactful journeys in my life, it didn't include Alana.

When we left the Grants, I experienced a despondent melancholy. What I had shared with the Grants belonged in the past. They had changed and I had changed. I would not see them again and I knew it.

I apologized to Alana, more from my own disappointment than hers, and resolved to just let matters take their own course for the remainder of the trip. Our plans were loosely constructed as was customary for the way we traveled together. We had a map of Ireland and a month to travel together before returning to Oxford. Both of us felt drawn to the coastal landscape of western Ireland. Otherwise, we had no formal itinerary.

Schull was close by and so, with no greater plans in front of us, we drove into the village, deciding to take a pint and a bit to eat at a local pub where we could sketch out a rough strategy for the next couple of days. The pub was filled with locals and given the obvious fact that Schull was not normally on the beaten path of tourists, we were clearly a curiosity. We sat at the bar and ordered a couple of pints and a shepherd's pie to split. Alana became engaged in a conversation with a gentleman to her left, who turned out to be a portrait artist for the Royal Family. On my right, also at the bar, I found myself in conversation with a newspaperman who claimed he wrote for the IRA underground newspaper. Soon the four of us moved to a table where we could visit. After telling them our disappointment in finding Gabe's Pub closed, the two men looked at each other as though we were both daft.

"Bloody hell man, I know Gabe's Pub. Today is half-Thursday. The pub is open at half day. It'll be open now. Come now, we'll all go to the pub together."

The portrait artist and newspaperman traveled together. It seemed a bit strange that the politics that might have separated the two men were clearly laid aside for this campaign. We would later discover that the two men had grown up together as young boys and this personal friendship trumped the political turmoil of the day.

The plan was simple enough. Alana would enter Gabe's with the two men and take a table. I'd wait about ten minutes and enter the pub, take a seat at the bar, order a pint, and then surprise Gabe. I was certain he would not recognize me. I looked considerably different than I had the first time I stepped into his pub.

Gabe's was pulsing. I took a stool at the end of the bar. Gabe was pulling drafts and gave me a nod as though to say, I'll be with you in a moment. In short time he was in front of me where he plunked down a Murphy's Irish Stout beer coaster to the patron next to me and asked for my order. He did not recognize me as I could easily pass for a local. I had on a heavy cable-knit sweater and tweed cap.

"T'what'll it be now?"

"The regular, please," I replied, watching a curious smile begin to form on his face.

"That would be a Murphy's, wouldn't it?"

"You would be correct."

"And, if I'm not grossly mistaken," he continued, "t'wouldn't it be Jeff Metcalf from Salt Lake City, Utah, now, would it?"

"That it would," and I smiled, reaching over and taking Gabe's hand into mine. He in turn leaned over the bar and gave me a hug.

"Glory be to God, Jeff! You've returned! How old would you be now? Tirty-two, tirty-three?"

"Thirty-two and you don't look a day older, Gabe."

"Michelle," Gabe called into the back kitchen, "Michelle, quickly now. You'll never believe who decided to pay us a call. Jeff Metcalf all the way from Salt Lake City, Utah."

Michelle came into the bar, wiping her hands on a dish towel, slid around the bar and gave me a kiss on the cheek and a warm embrace. "You are a sight for sore eyes," she offered up, "and a man of your word!"

I quickly explained the day's events and took them to the table where I introduced them to Alana and both men.

"This calls for a celebration!" exclaimed Gabe. "Do you like seafood, Alana?" he asked.

"Very much so," Alana replied, being immediately drawn into Gabe's enthusiasm.

"Then we'll head to Baltimore and eat at Chez Youen's."

"It's a rather lovely French restaurant with fabulous seafood," Michelle confided to Alana and further offered, "and the owner can be a bit of a grump but it is clearly worth it."

"Right now, everybody, please." Gabe was calling for his patrons' attention. "Everybody, if you will. Our friend and his lovely girlfriend Alana have just arrived from Salt Lake City, Utah, and we are going to go for a night on the town. So, rather than close the pub down, pay what you have consumed to the basket at the end of the night." And then he asked one of the locals to lock up the pub at half-ten.

Just like that and we were off to Baltimore, Ireland, for dinner.

We followed Gabe and Michelle in our Renault, winding along on tight country roads. The night was on.

"Nobody in the states would ever close a bar like that," Alana said, marveling at Gabe and Michelle's trust in the locals.

"Not in a million years. There'd be nothing left, would there?"

"It's just different here." I was beginning to get the feeling that, once again, by keeping ourselves open to the world, adventures happened.

By the time we reached the restaurant, clouds had darkened in front of us and were moving toward the restaurant. The wind picked up dramatically and the sky began spitting rain. We quickly dashed to the front door and entered. Stepping inside Chez Youen's, we instantly felt comfortable. If it was French or attempting to be French, it wasn't like anything resembling the many restaurants we had frequented in France. It was warm and inviting; a large fire crackled in the hearth and the interior felt very much a locals' spot. After meeting the owner/chef, Mr. Youen, we ordered a bottle of scotch to begin the evening properly. This was, in that wonderful hindsight one has the next day or several years later, probably a mistake. Then we talked.

Chef Youen was given permission by Gabe to create the evening for us and soon seafood began to appear at the table, each dish more succulent than the previous. By the time the main entrée arrived, we were well on our way into an evening of drink. I had forgotten just how good a storyteller Gabe was and he regaled us with the comings and goings of Ballydehob.

The featured dish was Coquilles St. Jacques in a white cream sauce with chanterelle mushrooms and a light green salad on the side. It was beyond anything I had ever tasted before and it has been the measure of every order of scallops since. Bottles of wine kept each course company and we were all soon elevated.

Outside, the storm deepened and high gale-force winds thrashed against the restaurant. We were the only patrons in Chez Youen's and, given the sudden nastiness and intensity of the storm, it was almost certain we would close the restaurant by ourselves.

Next door, on the pub side of the restaurant, we kept, or it seemed as though we kept, hearing the occasional sound of animals and the buffered sounds of voices. Because of the night, because of the foul weather, and because of the amount of drink we'd had, and because the conversation at the table was so engrossing, it was easy to dismiss until there was a heavy crash and the high-pitched neigh of a horse. It stopped conversation immediately and we looked at each other with raised eyebrows. Youen came storming out of the kitchen, swearing rapidly in French and headed directly and urgently into the pub.

When he returned to the dining area he approached our table. In his hand, a bottle of Cognac and five snifters. He placed the glasses on the table and poured us all a generous amount. In his French/Irish all he said to Gabe and Michelle was, "D. D. O'Driscoll is here tonight."

The name meant nothing to Alana and me, but Gabe and Michelle were clearly impressed or, perhaps more accurately, struck by the news.

"He's a healer," Michelle said. When we looked to each other, Gabe elaborated.

"You know, the seventh son of a seventh son."

Still nothing. "You have them in the states, don't you now?" Michelle asked, and the quizzical look on our faces called for further explanation.

"D. D. O'Driscoll is a famous healer in these parts. When he comes to town, any town in the south here, people come from miles to him for his healing powers. People and animals. They bloody flock to him and he takes pay in any form although he prefers drink and cold cash."

"He's particularly famous for his powers on the horses," interrupted Gabe.

"So we weren't imagining?"

"Not in the least. It's really something, isn't it?"

As luck or great misfortune would have it, and even over all these years the question has not been resolved, D. D. O'Driscoll ended up the night sitting and drinking with us until the early, early hours of the morning.

When he first sat at the table, his accent was so thick and heavily weighted by a rural Irish brogue, we had great difficulty understanding him. I think he could say the same of our middle-American accent. As the night wore on and the stories deepened, Alana claimed our accents completely disappeared and we gradually assumed each other's tongue.

To this day, we are both embarrassed and horrified to claim that we drove back to our B&B under the great influence of alcohol. I can say this without any exaggeration. We drove slowly, not because under the conditions it was a prudent thing to do, but because the storm was of hurricane proportion. The power to many communities had been severed. Under any circumstance we should not have been behind the wheel of our Renault, but we were.

At one point on the road along the coastline, a giant rogue wave crashed over a rock wall barrier and the Renault shuddered and then conked out. It terrified us to no end. Thankfully, the car turned over and we continued, but our laughter diminished and we became fully and completely focused on making it to Bantry Bay where we'd made accommodations for the night. The proprietress had not given us a key, so it required that we ring the doorbell at half-three. She was not in the least amused or pleased.

In the morning, we got up early, took tea, toast, eggs, bangers, and grilled tomatoes. After apologizing profusely to the owner, we stepped outside to take a walk along the quay. What we envisioned of Bantry Bay and what we saw were two very completely contrary images. Several boats had been crashed together, having come unmoored during the storm. A man in a tweed cap, cable-knit sweater, and black rubber galoshes stood on water in the middle of the harbor looking directly at us. It was such an overwhelmingly bizarre image that I felt compelled to call out to him. There was no dingy or any other boat nearby to explain how this had come to be.

"That's impressive," I called out, "Walking on water!"

"If I had that power," he yelled back, "I'd call me boat from the depths of this bay. I'm standing on the smoke stack of me fockin' boat!"

"Do you need help?"

"None that could be offered," he called back.

Quietly, upon our return to the B&B, we packed up our kit and drove off to continue our journey along the west coast of Ireland. We were lucky and we both understood this.

The night could have easily unfolded in a potentially catastrophic series of events; instead, it played out in a moment of magic catalogued deeply in our collective memory.

Three Down

I would like to say that I came to fly-fishing in a heralded way; that my grandfather handed down his split-cane rod to my father who, in turn, passed it on to me when I came of proper age. That, on any given summer evening we had, all three of us, walked the banks of the Beaverkill River casting to rising trout, finding ourselves alone at the pocket water of Horse Brook Run, a blanket hatch of Black Caddis and Blue Quill on the golden light of an early summer evening.

And further in this dream, on the way to the river, the men would encourage me to run ahead, the empty wicker basket slung across my back bouncing rhythmically against my hips so I could have the first shot at filling the creel with plump trout for dinner. My grandfather, Pops, and my father, Jack, would lazily walk the banks, pulling from their flasks and smoking Camel cigarettes. Sometimes, over my backcast I could see them watching me. It was a great feeling, as though I had been secretly inducted into their world, a world of smoke and alcohol, rivers and trout. It's the story I would like to tell but it would be far from the truth.

Instead, the year was 1968, in the small college town of Logan, Utah. It was a crisp winter night and the temperature held tight at five degrees. There was an illegal card game being held in a cramped room in the High Rise dorm. There was alcohol and cigar smoke and plenty of testosterone. It was strictly illegal for any of this to take place but the floor jock, Burr, had weightier problems on his mind.

The North Vietnamese had launched the Tet Offensive and the North Koreans had just hijacked the USS *Pueblo* three days earlier. Burr was a member of the active reserve for the U.S. Navy and worried he might be called up immediately for duty. He'd mentioned this bit of information to a bunch of us the day before at the mess hall. It was a critical mistake to offer this possibility to a group of immature young men.

That Friday following several hours of drinking beer at the Bistro in downtown Logan, three of us sent him a Western Union telegram ordering to report back to his unit in New Jersey for active duty.

At the front desk of the dorms, Lug Nuts told us Burr had been activated and was already packing his duffle bags. Rumor was that he'd booked a ticket on a Greyhound bus and would be heading for the East Coast to see his girl before shipping out. The joke had gone over the top and somebody had to tell him, probably me since it had been my idea. But the poker game was on.

Several hours into the poker game, Lump interrupted the usual banter, "Hey, anybody got any Drambuie? We're out."

"No, but I'll bet Burr has some," I offered. Since I'd folded early on the hand, I volunteered to walk down the hall to his room and borrow some.

Outside the door, I could hear the Irish Rovers rendition of "The Drunken Sailor" playing on his stereo. I knocked on the door. Nothing. On the second knock, he opened the door. His eyes were raw and puffy as though he'd been crying.

"Jesus, Burr, what's going on?"

"Want a drink?"

"Sure." I entered. The ashtray on his night desk spilled over with cigarette butts. He poured a healthy Irish whiskey in a jelly jar and handed it to me. He gestured for me to sit down.

"Did you hear what happened to me?"

"Yes," I answered.

"How fucked is that?"

"It's fucked."

Before I could say anything, he handed me a stack of albums, Tower of Power, Motown, The Chieftains, and my favorite Irish Rovers' collection.

"For you."

"I can't take these," I said, backing away. He pushed the albums into my hands.

"Bullshit. You've been a good friend."

"I haven't, Dick."

He stared at me, and for a moment, I thought he'd figured things out.

"I'm the one who sent that telegram to you."

He didn't believe me. "Tell me you didn't, Metcalf. That's not funny," he said, smiling. "It's really not funny."

"I know," I said. "I'm very sorry."

He stared at me for the longest time. I bent over and put the albums down on his bed. When I stood up, I was prepared for anything he could dish out. Whatever it was, I deserved it. He took the glass from my hand. I braced myself. It was swift and brutal.

"Leave my room."

"Dick, I don't know how to . . ."

"I will never talk to you again, Metcalf. Ever."

And he didn't.

When I finished telling the story to the boys around the table, Pin, a thug from Boston, simply said, "Fuck him if he can't take a joke." I was not overly fond of Pin.

"You didn't have to tell him," I shot back. "You chicken shitted out of it."

"Because it was your idea!"

I had not been playing poker well that night. I bought cards I had no right to buy, folded too early, made bad bets, bluffed when I shouldn't have. Pin's dismissal of my confession to Burr brought me back, though. In the next hour I'd gained back most of my losses; enough so that I could hold out against anyone at the table if need be.

On what would eventually turn out to be the final hand of the night, I drew an ace and jack down with the Big Casino up on the first three cards. A long-shot straight. I couldn't tell much by looking at the table. Lump from San Diego showed a queen, Vegas a jack, and Pin, the king of spades. Pin bet big. I guessed him for a pair. The other players, nothing of note showing, stayed with the first bet.

My next card was an ace up, so I had a pair of bullets. It was my bet so I began with Pin's previous bet. Nobody folded and when it came to Pin, he raised the bet, which, in turn, was called and raised again. The pot was building. I figured Pin for a pair of kings, which gave me the better hand, but since I didn't see any kings on the table, he could possibly have "trip" kings. I'd stay in for another card.

Around the table, cards were flipped and Pin drew a king that paired him on the table. He was exuberant.

"Fold boys . . . fold while you can!"

I drew a ten of spades, which gave me two pair, the dead man's hand. But, unless I'd misread the table, I still had the edge on Pin. He was bluffing. Absolutely going to try and muscle his way in and take the pot.

Wart, with trips on the table, bet. He was called and then raised heavily by Pin and in turn raised by Vegas, called and then raised by me. It was the first time Pin had actually paid attention to anyone other than himself and now he was forced to match the raises or fold. He stayed.

The pot was staggering for our normal sloppy, Friday night poker game. Stickler was the only one who had sense enough to fold. There were still six of us in the game. Pin gave himself away. He had a slight "tic." Whenever he was uncertain about his cards, he'd clench his teeth so tightly his jaw muscles would flex and pulse.

The next card was down and I drew the ace of diamonds which gave me a "full-boat." I could not see anything that would beat aces and tens on the table so I bet the max. I was in the perfect spot at the table. Pin should have dropped but I'd gotten under his skin.

"What do you think you've got going, Metcalf?" he snarled.

"Pay to play, Pin. Pay to play." I remained calm and that incensed him.

"Two pair won't do it . . ." For a moment, he hesitated and then called the bet. "Looking for a boat on the final card, on the last card, huh? It better be a life boat."

The players all laughed and I just nodded. The final card down caught me by complete surprise. Never in my life, before or since that night, have I ever had such a hand. It was an ace of hearts. Four honest aces, three of them down.

When my turn to bet came, I matched the pot. Chatter at the table stopped and those players in looked carefully, probably for the first time, at my hand. A pot raise was a big deal. "I don't know what you've got down, Metcalf, but it's too rich for my blood," Wart said, and folded.

Pin was the only player left at the table. The tension was thick.

"How much we got in the pot?" he asked, looking at about five dollars' worth of chips in his own stack.

"One hundred twenty-three dollars and change," Stickler said, and then added, because he wasn't particularly fond of Pin, either, "Pay attention, asshole."

My cash was already on the table. It was all the money I had left for January and February expenses.

"Are you folding?"

"What do you have, Metcalf?"

"Because I like you so much I'm going to tell you. I have four of the most beautiful aces you've ever seen and three of them are down under." That was all it took.

"Four aces! My big fat ass you do! I'll call."

"Match the pot," Vegas said.

"I'm going to have to go light," Pin replied.

"We don't play that way and you know it," Stickler said, "Either put the money down or Metcalf takes the pot."

"I'm short on cash." There wasn't a sympathetic smile at the table.

I didn't want Pin to fold. I wanted him to see those aces but I couldn't let him go light because I'd never see the money. I wanted to wipe the "smug" off his face.

"I don't have the cash right now. What if I put up a hundred and twenty-five dollars' worth of sports equipment?" he asked.

"Like what?"

"A West Yellowstone fly-rod, a Shakespeare reel, a vest with some flies, and a pair of Red Ball waders."

"That don't make it," Stickler replied.

"It's up to Metcalf. It ain't up to you."

"Go get the gear."

"I'm not going to need to," he said.

"If you don't, asshole, the game is over," Stickler snarled. It was getting heated.

"Are you serious? You want me to go down to my room and bring the gear back up so I can turn around and take it back down? Are you out of your mind?"

Pin slid his cards to Vegas to watch while he retrieved his fishing gear. When he returned, he threw the gear into the corner. "There you go. I call."

I turned my cards over exactly as they had been dealt to me. At the full-boat, the boys went wild. Aces and tens.

"That's a cool hand," Stickler said clapping me on the back.

Pin didn't say a thing for a few moments and then said, "What's the seventh card?"

"I told you already. It's an ace. Trust me, you don't want to see it."

"Turn the card over, asshole. I paid to see it."

When I did, Pin lunged over the table at me. He took a wild swing at me but was off balance. The boys jumped on him and kept us separated. I did not relish mixing it up with Pin. He outweighed me by at least forty pounds and was a good six inches taller.

The game broke up and I took the gear to my room where I stashed it in the closet. I went into the bathroom to brush my teeth before turning in and Burr was standing at one of the sinks shaving.

"I just had the poker hand of my life," I offered awkwardly, "Four aces, three down. Kicked Pin's ass."

Burr wasn't partial to Pin in the least so I thought this tidbit might get a smile out of him. Perhaps a snatch of conversation. Instead, he wiped the lather from his face, picked up his toilet kit and walked right by me as though I didn't exist.

Bullard's Bar

I began my college career at Utah State University. Like many young people of the day I was unsettled. It's clear now that I was not ready for college. I was too restless and immature. My edges were too sharp.

The political climate of the country was discomposed. The nation seemed on the brink of implosion and we all felt it. John F. Kennedy, Malcolm X, the Cold War, Martin Luther King Jr., the Selective Service, violent antiwar demonstrations across college campuses, Canada, North Korea, and the increasing escalation in Vietnam.

By the end of my first, very unimpressive year at university, I wanted to disappear and become as invisible as possible. For many reasons, legitimate and imagined, I could not return home. Because Utah State University was an agricultural school with an extremely well respected School of Forestry, the United States Forest Service placed ads around campus looking for adventurous young men who were interested in spending summers fighting forest fires. It sounded rough and tumble with an edge of romanticism to it. *The lone wolf setting out into the wilderness to test himself against the elements.* Baptism under fire. What could appeal more to a scrappy, disoriented dreamer? I applied for a position, was called back for a second interview, and was hired and assigned to USFS Fire Team in Bullard's Bar, California, deep in the Tahoe National Forest. At the end of the school year, I managed to hitch a ride with a college roommate who agreed to take me as far as Nevada City. From Nevada City, I was on my own.

I liked the size of Nevada City. It was an old California Gold Rush town, famous for the legendary Deer Creek find in the mid-1800s, and there were still a number of Victorian homes and historic buildings, mostly in disrepair, but I got a sense of what it must have felt like in its heyday. Tall pines surrounded the city and when the breeze blew, a sweet fragrance brushed the dusk. What struck me most that first evening was how dangerously dry and hot the evening air seemed. I understood the tinderbox possibilities of a high fire index, and for the first time since entertaining the notion of becoming a firefighter, I questioned what I was doing.

That night, after having tucked my duffle bag in a safe location where I was certain nobody would find it, I made my way to a saloon on Main Street and ordered a draft beer, a hamburger with fries, and a pickled hard-boiled egg. The last food I'd eaten was with a Basque sheepherder the day before and I wolfed the food down. It was a weekday night and the bar was dead, so I got visiting with the bartender and barmaid. When I finished telling them that I'd come out west to fight forest fires, they regarded me as though I was crazy.

Star, the barmaid, had a boyfriend who she thought was working pretty close to the same base camp where I would be stationed. "Maybe you guys will get to meet each other and work on the same crew. Wouldn't that be cool?" We would and it wasn't.

Manny, the bartender, asked me what kind of car I drove because Bullard's Bar was in "bumfuck Egypt" and the logging roads were pretty rough. "If them loggers don't kill you in their pickups, them stupid sons-a-bitches working on the dam will." When I explained that I didn't have a car and was planning to hitchhike to Bullard's Bar, Manny and Star were stupefied.

"Do you have any idea where you are fucking headed? It's a shit hole. There's nothing there. Nothing." Manny poured me a draft and plunked it down on the table. Before I could protest, he waived me off, "On the house, kid."

Star was a little more empathetic. Maybe if her boyfriend was coming through he could pick me up but she doubted he'd be driving to Nevada City until the beginning of the week. "He doesn't like to stay at the camp if he doesn't have to. It's pretty remote."

The romance of living out in the wilderness fighting fires was beginning to lose some of its appeal, and the reality that it might be one long and lonely summer was digging in. In some fantasy world, I had wrapped a pretty damn good story around my head. I was working in the Tahoe National Forest and I was going to be fighting forest fires. (True.) I imagined I would be working by Lake Tahoe and bikini-clad young women who thought it was just "peachy" to meet a big, strong firefighter, would surround me and beg me to go out with them. (False. False. False.) Judging by Manny's and Star's response, I'd be lucky if I saw a woman all summer long.

The cold fact was that I was stuck without a car and there was virtually no chance of making it to Bullard's Bar by hitchhiking. I'd probably miss my first day of work and I'd be fired and that couldn't happen. It just couldn't. I had no money to my name. My dream was to keep my head down and work hard all summer long and return home with a pocketful of money.

"Hey, Manny," Star asked, "What's that name of that sweet old guy who eats at the café every Sunday?"

"What old guy?"

"The guy that retired from the L.A. Fire Department. He works up there, don't he?"

Manny racked his brain but drew a blank.

"You know, the guy that looks like Popeye."

"Austen!" Manny shouted as though he'd won the jackpot. "Emerling. Austen Emerling, but he goes by 'Ace.'" He was pretty pleased with his power of recall.

"Maybe Ace could give him a lift?"

"He don't work at Bullard's Bar. I think he's out of Campton-ville or Dobbins. But it's kinda in the same area. Closer than you're going to get any other way."

"Why don't we go to the café and see if he's there tomorrow. What's he got to lose?" Star asked.

Manny shrugged.

That night I slept in the back of Manny's pickup truck. He'd rigged it up with a large cardboard box from a refrigerator that he folded in half and dropped in the pickup bed so I wouldn't feel the truck's ribs. When I gave up fighting the idea that taking this job was a monumental mistake, I settled down. After all, what did I really have to lose? I'd managed to get myself placed on academic and social probation during my first year of college. Having a summer to think things over might be just what I needed. I was headed nowhere fast and I knew it.

The night air was cool and sweet. On my back, tucked into my sleeping bag with a Levi jacket under my head as a pillow, I stared up at the constellations and thought about the kindness I'd been shown by these strangers. I wondered, if the situation were reversed, would I have offered myself up so easily? Would I have put a complete stranger up in my backyard? Probably not. Their generosity filled me with a sense that things might somehow work out.

Emerling was indeed Popeye. Star had offered a perfect description. He was five-foot-eight, compact, muscular, and sported a close-cropped crew cut. His hair was salt-and-pepper and his forearms could have been Popeye's. The only thing missing was the sailor's cap, a crude anchor tattoo, and a corncob pipe. When I shook his hand it was like being pinched in a vise.

My timing couldn't have been better. When we stepped into the café Ace was at the counter paying his bill. Star just came right out and asked him. We talked a bit but I think he agreed to give me a lift more for Star than for me. Star was hard to resist.

"Follow me, kid. I'm parked on the side of the café." Ace was headed to a trailer park where he lived with his wife during fire season. It was near enough to Bullard's Bar that it wouldn't be much of an inconvenience to drop me off at base camp. I quickly thanked Manny and Star for their kindness while Ace went back to drop off a tip.

I promised Manny and Star that I'd return at the end of the summer and let them know how things turned out. Star gave me a quick hug and I made small talk with Manny.

"Ready, kid?"

"I am, Mr. Emerling."

"Call me Ace."

"Yes, sir."

"Ace. Not sir."

"Ace."

I threw my kit into the back of Ace's truck and climbed into the cab.

"You're a college boy, right?" Ace asked.

"Yes."

"Then answer me this. Why do woodpeckers fly backwards?"

It felt like a bad *Knock Knock* joke.

"I don't know, Ace. Why do woodpeckers fly backwards?"

"So they can cool off their assholes," he cackled. "Get it?"

"I get it."

"Remember that joke. You'll need it this summer. It's going to be a hot one."

It was so stupid that I couldn't help but laugh, partly because it was so childish, partly because it was some comic relief, but more, I suspected, because Ace thought it was absolutely hilarious.

Ace was right. It was going to be a "hot one" and I would need that joke more than I could ever possibly know.

Cooking Lesson

If the cook hadn't been shot and killed in a barroom fight during a season of firefighting in California, I would never have stepped in front of a stove. But we were in a fix. Bob Riley, our fire boss, didn't look happy when he gathered our sad-sack faces together on the tarmac outside the bunkhouse.

"Okay, boys, here's the fuckin' facts. Cookie is dead and I'm not your mother. So if none of you can cook, you're going to starve to death. Period."

We stood around in a circle and stared dumbly at each other. Hambone, our tank truck operator, would be a disaster in the kitchen. Turkman, who hailed from Yakima, Washington, didn't throw his hand into the air and I thought he might because he came from farm country and this kind of made sense to me. Bugsy had a hard time remembering to zip his fly up and keep his shirttail tucked in, and Woody was always stoned or so we all expected. The older members of the fire crew lived off the hill. Ace lived with his wife in a trailer park outside Camptonville, Riley had government housing and he always emphasized that his "goddamn dinner" was always on the table waiting for him when he got home. God only knew where Patterson lived but judging by his size, we knew he wouldn't starve to death. He was a local boy and got fed real well. I wasn't about to stick my hand in the air because other than making pretty damn good grilled-cheese sandwiches with two thrift store irons in the college dorm, I knew nothing about cooking.

"One of you worthless sacks of shit better step forward. I want you fed and fed and well fed. I don't want any of you keeling over in firefight because you haven't had anything to eat and if you've noticed, there ain't no place within forty miles of here to get a meal."

In fact, our crew was truly stuck in the middle of nowhere. For entertainment we had a horseshoe pit, a basketball backboard, and then, of course, killing rattlesnakes. Every once in a while one of the other fire crews would come over for a barbecue and a basketball game and that would always turn into a brawl. It's how we released steam and it was expected. By the end of the night we were all pretty drunk, arm in arm shouting out our loyalty to the USFS and each other. We had to stick together because whenever we'd all roll into Nevada City or Grass Valley to get tanked up at a bar, there was always the very distinct possibility that we'd end up fighting either the loggers or the construction workers from the Pereni Dam project. The loggers and construction workers were in agreement about one thing and only one thing: they hated the United States Forest Service and everybody connected with it. So we were always attentive.

"There's a lot of ways you can get yourself killed in this business," Riley said, "lightning strikes, trying to outrun a fire, widow makers, asphyxiation, flare ups, rattle fucking snakes, but while I'm in charge, it's not going to be from starving. Now, who the fuck knows how to cook?"

There were still no takers. When Riley said the cook got off two hours early to prepare dinner and two hours additional pay, I raised my hand.

"So you can cook, college boy? Really? A college boy like you?"

"Yes, sir."

"And where did you learn to cook?"

"The Waldorf Astoria."

That stopped Riley cold. He smelled a rat, but he was caught off guard and didn't know where to go with this. It didn't take long for him to push me.

"Doing what?"

"Line cook and prep line," I answered, certain he'd fillet me on the spot.

"Well boys, it seems we have a cook, Chef Jeff! Now ain't that poetic. Chef Jeff."

And that it was except for the fact I had no experience at all and if I would have had my head screwed on tight, I would have backed out immediately. But, baited by Riley and knowing the seriously unimaginable tasks he would find for me as punishment if he felt I'd been playing him, I stared straight forward and didn't bat an eye.

"You start tomorrow, Chef. I don't care what slop you feed these guys but I want them full. Do you understand me?"

"Yes, sir, I do."

That night, when the crew turned in, I climbed out of bed and went into the kitchen. There wasn't much in the way of food in the freezer and enough in the fridge to maybe get us through to the weekend. We had eggs, white bread, bologna, hamburger, a couple of blocks of cheese, mustard, ketchup, mayonnaise, and some cold cuts. Other than some flour, peanut butter, canned fruit, and canned peas, the cupboards were bare. My job would require me to prepare breakfast, lunch, and dinner for six regulars. I did the math. One hundred and twenty six meals a week. At best, in a pinch, I knew how to make four dinner dishes. This was going to be a serious problem.

Getting back into bed, my roommate Turkman whispered, "You never cooked at the Waldorf, did you?"

"No," I confessed.

"Then why did you tell Riley you knew how to cook?"

"Because he enjoys making us feel stupid."

"But you lied to him and to us."

"I know."

"You've gotta tell Riley."

"Is that right?"

"Ya, because we need somebody that can cook."

"I've got it covered."

"I don't think so."

"Think what you like. If you don't like my cooking by the end of next week, you can take over as cook."

"I can't cook. I didn't put my hand up."

"Then shut the fuck up, Turkman."

I survived the week cooking some of the most unimaginably gross dishes. Grilled bologna and cheese sandwiches with macaroni and cheese for dinner, and another Ring Ding Dingy was a combination of several cans of Campbell's Tomato Soup (without the water) blended together with Velveeta cheese and slathered over Hoagie buns.

On my first trip into Nevada City to purchase groceries, I dropped into the saloon to see Manny and Star and perhaps pick their brains on a couple of dishes I might be able to cook for the crew. When I entered the bar, it took a second for my eyes to adjust. Tammy Wynette's "Stand by Your Man" was cranking out of the jukebox.

"Hey, kid," chuckled Manny. "You're still alive."

"Barely, Manny, just barely."

"Been on any fires? Been in any danger?"

"A few small fires. Nothing big. But I did something pretty dangerous."

"What's that, kid?"

"I put my hand up to be the cook. Ours got killed."

"We heard about it over here. Didn't know him."

"So, they needed a cook and I put my hand up."

"Kid, the first rule is: never put your hand up. Didn't you learn that from college?"

Star came in the front door, grabbed her half-apron, wrapped it around her waist, and caught me gawking at her.

"Well, look who's here," she said, smiling broadly. "You didn't quit, did you?"

"I'm in town to buy groceries," I answered.

"He stuck his hand up," Manny chided, "now he's the camp cook and HE don't know how to cook."

Star looked at me, amused. "Why would you go and do something like that?"

"Because the cook gets off two hours before everybody else."

"And just how is that working out?" she asked, already knowing the answer.

"Not too well. I'm up a couple of hours before everybody in the morning to get breakfast and lunch set up. I never get to bed at a reasonable hour. I'm burning it on both ends and that's not good."

"You've got to figure it out, kid, or those guys will kill you."

"I know. I don't even know where to begin. Do you have any cookbooks I could borrow?"

"Kid, we don't use cookbooks."

"Manny, do we still have *The Joy of Cooking* in the back?"

"I think so. It'd be back there somewhere."

"Can we give it to Jeff?"

"We ain't using it. Don't see why not."

Star disappeared into the kitchen and returned with Bombauer and Becker's seminal cookbook, *The Joy of Cooking*. It was thumb-worn, with stains on the front cover and the odd paper marker sticking out of, I supposed, a favorite recipe.

"Here," she said, "it was my mom's."

"Jesus, Star," I argued, "I can't take this." I tried to push the book back into her hands but she wouldn't have anything to do with it.

"Just take it. You need it more than I do. We don't even use it."

"I'll bring it back at the end of the summer," I promised.

Although I didn't order anything, Manny plunked a cheeseburger down in front of me. It was slow in the bar, virtually empty, so both Manny and Star had time to visit with me, offer me advice.

Manny's advice on cooking and, more importantly, purchasing food was practical and down-to-earth, informed by years of experience in the kitchen. I scribbled notes while he rambled along. Simple things, like, "Ask for a discount on all your food on account of the fact you work for the USFS!" "Don't ask them sons-a-bitches what they want to eat for dinner. You ain't a fucking restaurant." And, "If them bastards don't like what you cook, let them go hungry." I would remember and use all of his advice during the summer. "Fire fighting is easy. Cooking is fucking hard work."

Star's suggestions were of a more practical nature but equally valuable. "Keep breakfast simple. Good and filling. Quick-drop biscuits and gravy is always a winner and easy to do. You can do the gravy the night before. You'll figure stuff out."

"Okay, great. Good. Thanks. This is really helping me out."

"For lunches, everybody makes their own."

"Great idea. I've been making all the lunches and everybody complains. Not enough mayonnaise. Too much mayonnaise. Thicker slices of cheese."

"Then don't make their lunches. That way you're not busting your ass for a bunch of ungrateful bastards."

"That makes sense."

"For dinners, pick a few simple recipes until you get the hang of things. Do a corned beef and cabbage. It's cheap and filling. Maybe a creamed chicken over rice. Then the next week two more new dishes. Cook a ham. Meat's good here and you can use the leftovers. Pretty soon, you're cooking."

I'd driven into Nevada City looking for divine inspiration and I found it in the earthy, good-natured, and generous personalities of Star and Manny. On the way out of town I stopped by the public library, got a library card, and checked out every book I could find about cooking. While the other crewmembers read smut, I read cookbooks. And by the end of that summer, I was not just surviving—I was cooking some pretty damn good dishes and enjoying it. I began to feel comfortable enough to improvise in my cooking. I knew a place where I could pick wild asparagus and watercress so they started to appear on the table. It would never have happened without the courtesy of Manny and Star. They were true mentors and good friends, generous in their praise. It was funny, but the crew had changed their eating habits. Word got around and even Riley and some of the higher-ups would drop by if I were cooking dry-rubbed ribs. They'd often come under the guise of playing basketball against us. Over the summer, we frequently mixed it up with our bosses until the games got a little too violent. But the food and beer would always settle us down.

At the end of the fire season I gave everybody in the crew a couple of their favorite recipes written in longhand on index cards. It was like Christmas. Guys who were pretty happy with mac and cheese at the beginning of the fire season were now offering their own thoughts on my seasoning techniques. Hambone had offered some advice on the fact that my curried chicken could use a bit more splash, say, with Tabasco or Crystal sauce. Three months ago, Hambone didn't know curry from a hole in the ground and now he was a sous chef offering me advice. It was fabulous and I absolutely loved it. Every single mouthful of it.

Birds of Prey

The letter was straightforward Jones.

"We'll meet in Boise then drive to Kuna or maybe not. Put in on the water in my canoe and float Birds of Prey. I'm bringing my new girlfriend, Chris. You'll like her. Rain gear. It will rain. You bring dinner, snacks, etc., gear for a couple of days and I'll bring the rest."

There was a post-script. "P.S. If you snooze, you lose!"

Jones and I met a lifetime ago. At the time, he worked for Kennecott Copper as an environmentalist and I'd started an alternative education program in a local high school for at-risk students. Jones, along with another maverick, Paul Rokich, a Kennecott Copper employee who later was dubbed "Johnny Appleseed of Bingham Canyon" had begun a project to personally reforest the mountains attached to the great copper mine's holdings. At best, these two men were considered crazy, but in all likelihood, they were regarded as dangerous environmentalists. In our separate worlds, the three of us would be watched.

Beyond the madness of their endeavor, I liked the simple fact that these two men, vastly different from each other in all ways possible, shared a passion for the "wild." The idea that Jones and Rokich would consider the impossible plausible made perfect sense to me.

Similarly, I believed that big things could happen by small groups of teachers with limited means and great ideas. The rag-tag students I taught were outcasts, students who, for many reasons, hung outside the boundaries of traditional public schools. At the time, the possibility that these students might graduate and amount to productive citizens was just as preposterous a notion as saving the barren hills of the Oquirrh Mountains by planting trees.

The three of us formed an unholy alliance of sorts between the Kennecott environmental outcasts and the outcasts from Brighton High School. In the course of two years we planted several thousand Douglas fir trees, poplar and white fir seedlings. Being connected in a very physical way to the land changed the lives of all of us involved in the reforestation program.

When the copper company terminated Jones's position he moved to Boise, Idaho, to work for the Department of Mines. Our plan to remain connected with each other was simple. We'd take turns organizing backcountry trips. The rules were simple enough. One of us would plan the itinerary and the other person would just show up ready to play. The Birds of Prey canoe trip hatched from this promise. My assignment was the food.

Spring weather in the West is unpredictable. I met Jones and his girlfriend, Chris, at the appointed rendezvous. I liked Chris instantly. She was cut from the landscape and a perfect partner for this trip. After loading up the canoe, we pushed off for a day of bird watching. Angry clouds hung off in the distant sky and we were aware.

It took us time to adjust the weight in the canoe. Within the hour, the weather turned sour. First came the wind, followed by whitecaps on the water, spits of rain, and then a torrential downpour. Lightning forced us off the water. We sought shelter in an abandoned farmhouse that had, during the days of the early Mormon settlements along the Snake River, operated as a melon farm.

We were damp and shivering from the wet. A rusted Monarch stove occupied the heart of what was once the kitchen. Broken chairs and torn flooring provided us with enough kindling to get a fire going. We huddled around the small fire and sipped brandy. Occasionally, droplets of water dripped from the dipped and swollen ceiling above us and fell onto the heavy cast plates of the Monarch, hissing like rattlesnakes. The weather was relentless. Hailstones began to beat down on the tin roof in an angry cacophony of sound. Jones nodded for me to follow him to the front porch. We stepped outside and were pummeled by hailstones. A quick cut around the porch gave us shelter.

"What do you think?" he asked uncomfortably.

"I don't know."

"We've lost a lot of time. About three hours. Maybe more. Hard to tell."

"Where should we be?"

"Below Swan Falls."

"We'll have to get back on the water."

"I'm afraid so."

Before climbing into the canoe, we bailed water. Over our shoulders a black scowling sky. Conversation was at a minimum because we all knew the dangers of being on the water in such circumstances. It was foolish.

The Snake, normally smooth and meandering, was choppy with whitecaps. Chris seemed shaky getting into the canoe.

"Are you doing okay?" I asked.

"I'm fine," she answered and then tucked into herself and pulled the poncho over her head.

We agreed to keep the canoe as close to shore as possible in case lightning exploded across the water. The wind picked up, pushing the canoe upstream. Paddling downstream against the storm, we continued to lose ground.

"We're going to have to pull the canoe downstream," Jones yelled.

"There's something very wrong with this picture," I replied.

Chris poked her head out of her poncho. "Do you need my help?"

"Just try to keep the canoe balanced," replied Jones.

We rigged nylon ropes to the bow of the canoe and mucked awkwardly through brackish foamy water trying to advance the canoe downstream.

A freakish twist in the wind pushed the stern of the canoe out into the main current and we had a difficult time holding on. A rogue wave hit the canoe broadside and Chris screamed. The canoe heeled at an alarming angle but her shear athleticism prevented it from capsizing.

"Dammit!" she yelled. "The food!"

Jones and I watched our Styrofoam cooler bob up and down as it disappeared into the main channel.

"Sonofabitch!" I yelled.

"Shouldn't we try to get it?" she called.

"No," Jones answered. It was all he could say.

Four hours later we pulled off the Snake and made camp on high ground above the boiling swirls. The weather had abated temporarily and we quickly pitched the tent, hauled our dry bags up the hill, slipping clumsily in the mud, and deposited them inside the tent.

"Chris," I asked, "did you bring any dry clothes?"

"I did."

"Why don't you change into them while Jones and I go looking for firewood."

"Okay."

"Stay warm. Stay inside the tent."

"Jones, let's split up. I'll go downriver. You go up."

"Sounds like a plan," Jones said, adding at the last minute, "Do you think she'll ever go out with me again?"

"I've been trying to figure out why she went out with you in the first place."

Finding dry wood would not be too much of a problem. Along the Snake River there were a number of abandoned farms with old barns bent and crippled, the siding grey and weathered. I found some dry kindling and some split logs on the underside of a collapsed tool shed. It was a bonanza. I scurried back to the campsite with the treasure.

I met Jones cresting the hill.

"Nothing upriver?"

"A bust. Where'd you get the wood?"

"Around the corner. There's a small tool shed with a pile of logs."

"The gods are with us," he said, smiling for the first time in a very long day.

"I'll drop this load off and come back."

"Great."

We passed each other on the return, Jones hauling a load that tucked under his chin. "There's not much left. Maybe half a load."

"I'll get it. Get a fire going and get into some dry clothes. Maybe try to convince Chris to go out with you again."

"Good idea."

When I got back to the shed, I took some time to look around this abandoned farm. I've always admired the scrabble-rock toughness and the rugged individualism of the men and women who moved across the country to seek out a new life. What must this have looked like on the first sighting? The Snake River with its broad chest, an elevated landscape off the water with rich soil where a small house could be built, an abundance of deer and rabbit. Would this not have been heaven by any measure?

Quite by happenstance, I glanced downriver to a back eddy of swirling water and was stunned to see the Styrofoam cooler swirling lazily in a circle. I rushed down the hill, found a branch and was able to manipulate the cooler to the bank. The duct tape I'd wrapped around the lid was still in place. I fully expected to peel back the top and find everything inside ruined. Instead, it was exactly the way I had packed it a couple of days ago. Lamb chops marinated in garlic, red wine, rosemary, ground rock salt, and pepper still tightly packaged in zip lock bags. There was shredded Romaine lettuce with bleu cheese crumbles, and a simple

oil-and-vinegar based dressing in a plastic bottle. I'd picked up
a loaf of Basque bread and two very good bottles of burgundy,
strawberries with a plastic cup full of a mixture of brown sugar
and sour cream, and two dark-chocolate candy bars.

Chris shrieked when she saw me carrying the cooler. Jones had
a great fire going and upon hearing Chris, stuck his head out of
the tent.

"Praise the RIVER GODS!" he yelled, crawling out of the
tent. He was in dry clothes now and once I deposited the food
by the fire, I changed into some old World War II wool surplus
pants and a green plaid Woolrich shirt. Grabbing our coffee cups,
we popped open the bottle of burgundy and toasted each other.

"We were lucky today," Jones offered.

Chris and I both nodded. For a while, the three of us just
stared into the fire, processing, I suspected, what might have happened had the world tilted slightly against us.

"I'm starved," Chris declared breaking the silence.

I'd tucked a half dozen coat hangers in the stern of the canoe
to roast the lamb. While I skewered the chops, Jones and Chris
opened the second bottle of wine and prepared the rest of the
meal. I grilled the chops over the coals, taking great care not to
overcook them. It began to snow lightly, a dry snow that dusted
the ground like confectioner's sugar. Jones and Chris pushed our
gear to the back of the tent, brought the food inside, and made
a spot for me to sit. I stayed outside until the lamb was ready to
be served.

We heaped up our plates with food and filled our coffee cups
to the brim with dark burgundy wine. Hail bounced off the roof
of the tent. We were alive and I suddenly felt very emotional about
the day; how it might have turned out and how, in fact, it did.

The events of the day could have been disastrously different.
We'd been lucky and we knew it. A missed stroke of an oar blade
at the wrong time could have made all the difference between us
being here or not. There is no room for fools in the wilderness.

"Oh my God," Chris moaned after her first bite of lamb. "Oh my God! I have never tasted anything so good in my life."

From the outside, a cinematographer would construct a wide-angle shot at the opening of a domed tent. Snow would be falling gently against the tent and three figures would be illuminated by the glow of a lantern hanging from a loop in the ceiling of the dome. Narrowing the distance to a close-up, the lens would reveal two men and a woman sitting shoulder to shoulder at the front entrance of the tent; wind-burned faces, their laps burdened under the weight of a plate full of incredible edible surprises.

There would be no dialogue at all and the audience would know that this was a perfect moment in the movie. It would have been impossible to decipher where and when this scene took place in the arc of the narrative, or whether something tragic might befall one of these characters following this scene, but in this instant, life on this spit of land along the Snake River was undamaged and pure.

I have carried this memory with me for over forty years and this snapshot, this recollection of the trip, has never dulled or varied from the script. I have lost track of both Chris and Jones over the ensuing years. It's that way in life.

But this story is a river's tooth, the pine-pitch knot of a rotted tree that does not disintegrate in the elements or with the passage of time and I can only hope, in this given moment, it was the same for my two tent mates.

Our Family Album

Recently, while teaching a poetry class to a group of nontraditional adult learners, I asked my students to bring in an old photograph that carried some sort of electrical charge, either positive or negative, which they could work into a poem. We'd read the hauntingly beautiful poem by Margaret Atwood, "A Photograph of Me," which begins as a very clear visual image of a country landscape. Perhaps at the narrator's home or family retreat. The clarity of the image changes halfway through the poem when she writes, "The Photograph was taken the day I drowned"—which distorts and blurs the lens so carefully focused in the first part of the poem. After a meaty discussion trying to unlock the secret code of this poem, the class, myself included, began creating our own poems using the photographs we brought to class.

The photograph I selected was a black-and-white picture of me with my arm around my sister, Sue. I explained to the class that as a kid growing up with a brilliant older sister who "actually did know everything," my sole purpose in life was to conjure up a way to dispose of my sister without leaving a trace or, if I had to leave a trail, it would lead directly to my younger brother, Barry, who was always a convenient scapegoat. The photograph was taken for our Uncle Bill who'd sent us birthday presents. My gift was a cool leather World War II bomber jacket and my sister received a dorky, linen Dutch-girl hat and a pair of wooden shoes. My mother insisted I put my arm around my sister, which

I refused to do even after several stern warnings, until my mother finally threatened to bring my father out from the house to make me do so. Reluctantly, I slipped my arm around her, but the look of disdain on my face is evident. It was the instant the photograph was snapped. My eyes are turned toward the heavens in the hope that divine providence might intercede on my behalf.

However, what is truly remarkable to me in this photograph is the look on my sister's face. Until that very moment in class when I asked my students to seriously study their own images for something they hadn't seen before, I did not realize I had never done so with this photograph. For the first time I noticed the absolute look of repulsion on her face, like perhaps, as inconceivable as it might sound, she was not particularly thrilled with me having my arm around her.

Sue's Point of View

I remember that photograph. At that moment, as the shutter snapped, I was concentrating very hard trying to remember the vanishing spell I had read about . . . *Eye of toad, toe of newt.* Something like that. In fact, the next photograph in the "Stupid Dutch Girl Hat Triptych" demonstrated that I was indeed able to make Jeff disappear completely, if only for a short time. He is absent in the picture and our father and younger brother are fading from view in the window. My magic was powerful if only temporary.

Despite the forced photographs taken with our arms around each other, I was every bit as fond of Jeff as he was of me—only I was less direct in my approach.

In truth, the moment I first laid eyes on my brother Jeff, my sole ambition in life was to "become an only child." From that day on, my energy was focused, my actions purposeful. I was determined. I was on my way.

Jeff proved to be more of a challenge than I expected. He was tough and resilient.

Jeff's Side

Shortly before my mother passed away, my sister brought the only album we have of our childhood to my home in Salt Lake City. Our parents were not, among other things, very diligent photographers. There are, of course, a number of photographs of us growing up until about the age of six or eight, and then beyond that really very few—almost as though we ceased to exist beyond the age of twelve and thirteen. Once, we traveled around the world on a single roll of film. At cocktail parties my parents would often tell this story as though it were a badge of honor. In truth, it was a sad omen of things to come.

Perhaps most haunting about revisiting our family album is the fact there are few images of a complete family. We could find precious few photographs of the five of us together. There are the odd few, but even in these, our family seemed very scattered and out of focus. In a sense, this defined the way we would live our lives— often out of focus, certainly out of touch, and, more specifically, disconnected from each other in the important matters of life. The death of our father and the declining health of our mother have forced us, in many ways, to begin the process of healing.

My sister is less than a year older than me. She was a crafty little villain, difficult to deal with, and was the master of getting even. My approach in trying to remove her from my life was always straightforward. I learned to take advantage of any weakness.

Sue had a deathly fear of needles. Once, while thumbing through a *National Geographic*, looking for pictures of naked women, I showed her a photograph of a Lutheran missionary giving a vaccination to a group of villagers somewhere deep in the Congo. No sooner did she look at the photograph than she fainted. At this point it is important to note that she did not fall lightly to the floor. It was a marvelous drop to the canvas, as though heavyweight Mike Tyson had cold-cocked a small child . . . something I fully think him capable of doing.

When she came to, her eyes rolled rubber around her head and she asked what had happened. I realized she seriously couldn't remember what precipitated the event so I immediately hustled off to the room and shared the news with my brother. We began searching through back issues of *Life* magazine in search of any pictures that contained needles. It didn't take us long to discover a couple of classic photographs. The first was a full-page photo of a nurse giving a polio vaccination to a plump little boy. The boy's face shows him on the verge of tears while in the background Dr. Jonas Salk looks on. In the second photo a long line of Korea-bound servicemen are receiving inoculations preparatory to boarding a navy ship bound for war. These were good—very good.

My brother was my apprentice assassin so it was important that I include him in on the subtleties of the craft. So on an evening when my parents were leaving for a cocktail party and my sister was drawing a bubble bath in our large, claw-footed tub, I gave my brother the nod.

We'd carefully rehearsed how this would go down. My brother would knock on the bathroom door. My sister would snap at him and tell him to get lost. I would have him pause for a moment and then tell Susan he was having trouble sounding out a word. My sister would huff and puff and then reluctantly agree to open the door. He would show her the picture and she would faint and we would have ourselves a grand laugh.

I left my brother at the door and ducked into the hallway where I could hear my parents giving instructions to our tender downstairs in the main foyer. I could hear my brother speak his lines. I could hear my sister moan. I heard the latch click open, as I knew it would, because my sister couldn't resist any opportunity to show off her academic superiority when it came to her two rather dumb brothers. I could hear the magazine pages rustle.

What I didn't expect to hear was a loud thump followed by the wind being knocked out of somebody. And it was a very loud thud, so loud, in fact, that both my parents heard it.

"What was that?" my mother cried.

"I don't know," I replied, but clearly something had gone wrong.

"I think," my brother screamed, "Sue killed herself."

I ran into the bathroom. I could hear my parents running up the stairs. I was scared to death. My sister had fainted, fallen back and cracked her head open on the tub. She had a gash on the back of her skull that bled onto the tile floor.

In a series of blinding movements my mother came to the rescue. She yelled at both of us to stand back. She told my father to get a cold rag and some ice cubes and she lifted my sister's head up carefully. Sue moaned and her eyes blinked open. My mother queried her.

"Did they do something to you?" she asked, looking over her shoulder at my brother who was still holding *Life* magazine.

I could only imagine what my mother was capable of doing to my brother. I probably should have told Mom that I put him up to showing Sue the photograph and she fainted, but I didn't. The life of an assassin is a dangerous one and my brother would simply have to take the fall by himself.

Sue regained her senses and looked at my brother and then looked at me. She knew. I knew. She knew I knew she knew. I was dead. It was clear that my brother couldn't have imagined all of this up on his own. All she had to do was speak my name and I would be dead. My mother compressed a wet rag filled with ice to the baseball now on the back of Sue's head. My mother repeated the question again.

"Did they do this to you?"

My lip began to quiver. I almost confessed but my training over the years taught me that nothing good would come from such an admission. Truth did not set you free; in fact, it usually got me a good old-fashioned ass whipping and a week of solitary confinement in my room.

"No," Sue answered. She looked directly into my eyes and said, "I slipped and hit my head on the tub."

I couldn't believe it. My sister had fallen so hard that she'd actually lost her memory. There was a God. Life was good.

However, my mother was not convinced.

"So help me God! If they had anything to do with this, just tell me."

"They didn't. Honest. I just slipped."

I do not, for a moment, think my mother believed my sister. But without an eyewitness, all she had was a mother's instinct and circumstantial evidence. It wasn't enough for a conviction. I knew the law.

My parents left for their cocktail party. My brother and I disappeared into our room where we began playing with our army soldiers on the floor. In a while, my sister came into the room without knocking.

"Hey! You're supposed to knock before coming in here. Read the sign on the door, or are you retarded now?" She breezed into the room without even acknowledging us.

"Both of you are going to clean my room every morning and make my bed before we go to school. You are going to do it every single day for as long as I want you to do so."

"Why would we do something that stupid?" I asked.

"Because if you don't, I'm going to tell mom what you did today." And she would, so we did. We got very good at making beds. We had plenty of practice.

Sue

I had an entire litany of incantations specifically directed at removing my brother from my life. Walking down the street I would step on any crack—every crack—chanting under my breath, "Step on a crack, break your BROTHER'S BACK!" Other chants were said openly with loud, heartfelt enthusiasm: "Cross your heart, hope to die, stick a needle in MY BROTHER'S EYE!" Despite an unusually large number of childhood mishaps, my brother remained intact. Or worse, in place.

Except for extreme circumstances, I pretty much gave up on magic and incantations. I turned to a higher spirit for guidance. For a while I became a pious and devout Catholic. I'd been assured by our parish priest, Father Vaigen, that God not only answered our prayers, but He forgave us for our sins. I read anything I could get my hands on pertaining to the lives and deaths of the saints. They were bloody stories; full of various ways martyrs had been (as I prayed my brother would be) dispatched. Since God did not respond to my prayers as quickly as I had hoped, I entreated the saints to "intercede" on my behalf and invite Jeff to join them in paradise.

Saint Simon Stylites was my favorite. Some kid in my catechism class told me that Stylites was the patron saint of flagpole sitters in medieval Italy. According to my source, to gain favor with Saint Simon, one prayed to him from a precarious location, like atop a refrigerator. I routinely assumed a perch on the family's Kenmore refrigerator whenever I sought intercession from Saint Stylites. My family, it seemed, had mistaken my intended fratricide for faith. They feared I would join a convent, become a nun. I preferred to get rid of my brother and become a convict. I was a minor and with time off for good behavior, it would be worth it.

Jeff

In ways, my sister's attention to religion proved to be a blessing in two areas. While my sister perched atop the refrigerator it gave me time to grub around in her bedroom unnoticed. It was in these moments that I learned to pick locks, something that would later help me a great deal in life. She had a pink-and-white-striped diary that I could pick open with a paper clip and read at leisure. Soon, though, I turned my attention to one of her favorite passions:

a collection of porcelain dolls. Not wanting to ignore my brother, I brought him into the room, handed him a pair of scissors, and turned him loose on Sue's collection. Undiscovered for the better part of the morning, he was able to shear the doll collection before being discovered by my mother. His punishment more than met the crime and since I had wandered into the kitchen to visit with my sister, I had a perfect alibi.

I also discovered that there is great wealth in religion. My sister's religious bent forced us to attend mass every Sunday. Our parents would drop us off at church, give us money to drop in the collection plate, and pick us up after Saint Sue had atoned for all her sins. I explained to my brother that we never put our money in the collection plate. This money went directly into our pockets to supplement our allowance. Then, I taught him the art of thumping the collection basket and swiping additional money as it passed down the pew. We became adroit at this craft and managed to purchase a rather large collection of comic books with this additional money.

Sue

Religion failed me. I tried the scientific method instead. Under the pretext of scientific experimentation, I prepared all sorts of noxious combinations for my brothers to imbibe or swallow. It was easy to convince them to participate in these experiments. They were always in a perpetual state of hunger and I knew from past experiences that sudden death by poison was more than I could hope to attain.

I read about cholesterol and the dangers of a diet filled with fats. I embarked on a campaign to become a death-defying cook. Thus, over the ensuing years, my brothers were treated to meals of, but not limited to, wallpaper paste porridge, hamburgers made from canned dog food, and, the heart attack special, white layer cake frosted with pure lard icing. They ate everything I put in front of them, particularly if I placed a small bet that they couldn't. My greatest disappointment was that not only did my attempts fail to bump them both off, they actually seemed to thrive on it.

Jeff

My sister doesn't give herself enough credit. Her recipe for dog food burgers was an absolute classic. I wasn't keen on the wallpaper porridge, it was a bit runny for my taste, but I can take nothing away from those burgers. By using Tabasco mixed in with canned corn and a host of other exotic spices, she produced what I believe to be the forerunner of Cajun-style burgers. I remember her as being an innovative cook—a person not afraid to experiment in the culinary arts.

In her own way, she probably had a great deal to do with developing my love of cooking. If she could do that with dog food, what else was possible?

Sue

As we both approached adolescence, it dawned on me that neither my hard work nor my virtue had an impact on shortening my brother's life span. In the same respect, my brother had not completed the task he set before himself.

Over the years, however, I'd developed a profound, albeit grudging, admiration for my brother's tenacity and for his ability to survive my best efforts to eradicate him from the face of the earth. He was a strong and, I was forced to admit, worthy adversary.

Eventually, I succeeded in my only childhood goal by leaving home. At the age of fifteen my parents dropped me off at the airport, wished me luck, and watched as my plane departed for Texas. I would attend Rice University where I received a degree in art history. Later I would marry, move to New Mexico, have a daughter, earn a law degree, and practice law. I had chosen, for many reasons, never to return home.

No formal truce was ever declared between my brother and me. The summer I left home, my brother was packing up to join a carnival. As a parting gesture, and to give him something to remember me by, I stuffed some outrageous underwear of mine into his duffle bag. He would later tell me, in that wonderful storytelling way of his, that the ex-cons he worked with took quite a liking to his style.

As we led our separate lives, our paths seldom crossed. Our family has always been sloppy that way. But over the years, I began to see my brother in a different light. When our children were born, close to the same time, I realized that Jeff was the genuine article. The very qualities that I detested in him as a sibling, such as his tenacity, his sense of humor, and his fierce independence in charting his own course, were now enviable assets in his role as a father. Unlike our parents and the parents I would see in my divorce practice, Jeff was relentlessly there for his kids, as he had been there for me.

Recently, as our mother's memory diminished, our family album has been the focus of some powerfully healing dialogue between Jeff and myself. We laugh about our childhood, the now-ancient hostilities, and try to imagine our own children's journey. What stories will they tell? I suspect, in a way, it is how we talk to each other about ourselves.

There are the words *brotherhood* and *sisterhood*, but neither one truly describes the relationship between Jeff and me. Walter Kelly (who wrote the cartoon *Pogo*) wrote, "We have met the enemy and he is us!" This might be a more accurate way of describing the two of us. Talking about the family album has helped me understand that Jeff and I know each other at our best and for our worst. You can't have many secrets from somebody who was potty-trained with you. And it forces me to admit that, in a way, Jeff was my first passion.

Surprise Wedding

The idea for a surprise wedding came to me in a blinding snow-storm. Literally. My girlfriend, Alana, and I had skipped town to Deer Valley ski resort for my birthday. Nothing big, nothing fancy. It was just what I wanted and we both needed. A quiet weekend, just the two of us.

Sitting in a luxurious hot tub in the living room of a multimillion-dollar condo, we watched snowflakes float across the valley floor. We sipped martinis, listened to music, and caught up on each other. I accidentally knocked over a bottle of Bombay gin that shattered on the tile floor. Alana suggested I stay put while she cleaned up the mess and then she would drive into town and pick up another bottle. I protested weakly and watched as she disappeared into the night.

While she was gone, I thought about us. The two of us had been hanging around together for three years. This was a woman who, when I took a sabbatical to Oxford for a year, didn't hesitate leaving a very successful job and rolling the dice with me. It was a great journey. This was a woman who gave me space when I needed it and reined me in when I got too far out on the edge. Alana was a woman I felt like I could be married to, but, and this was a big but, I'd been married before when I was very young and I was nervous about making such a commitment again. And, at the same time, I knew this made no sense whatsoever. It was my phobia and I was so affected by the fear that I couldn't even manage to say the "M" word. We'd had many conversations talking about the future, about maybe getting married when things seemed right. How right did things need to be? In truth, I was afraid. Terrified.

Looking out the window, I could just make out what I thought was Alana's car returning up the canyon. I decided to surprise her when she arrived so I wrapped a towel around my head like a turban and waited stark naked behind the front door. The condo was rather secluded so I thought it would be hilarious to jump out naked and shout "SURPRISE!" I waited until I heard her footsteps by the door and threw open the door, jumped out, and screamed, "SURPRISE!" My "SURPRISE" was immediately countered by a collective "SURPRISE" from ten of our best friends. The door locked behind me and Alana was without a key. All of us stood on the front porch, me stark naked, my nipples turning blue, while everybody laughed and Alana departed to find a security guard who could let us into the condo. Thankfully, a coat appeared and was able to cover up my nakedness.

That night we cooked a phenomenal dinner, drank extraordinary wines, and regaled each other about our favorite stories including, I'm embarrassed to admit, my own surprise at being caught naked in front of my friends. Several of us gathered outside to smoke cigars. It was there, at that precise moment, when something became very clear to me. In hushed breath, I announced, "We're going to get married."

"When?" B.T. asked.

"Maybe the end of January," I replied.

"You don't know?"

"No. Neither does she," I added, as if this might clarify matters. "I'm going to throw her a surprise wedding!"

The blank stares answered my question. A surprise birthday was one thing, but a surprise wedding? It was, by all accounts, unusual to say the least.

Between October of 1983 and January of 1984, I got schooled. Most of Alana's female friends thought I was stepping across the line.

How dare I take the excitement of planning a wedding away from Alana? What if she didn't accept my proposal? Just how did I think I could pull off something like this without her knowing about it? Didn't she actually need to go with me to file for a marriage license?

Good points. Good questions, but I plowed on.

Bill Nassikas, at that time the director of food and beverage at Deer Valley and a good friend, helped me plan out the wedding and menu. We would create a chapel in the Silver Lake Lodge where all the guests would be waiting. Under the guise of going to dinner at the Café Mariposa, we would order our dinner (which would never arrive) and find our way upstairs to the newly created chapel. The plan, however, had one missing part. How could we get Alana up from dinner and into the chapel without arousing her suspicions? Minor detail. We'd sort that out.

I needed an unusual band, one that nobody would expect, or forget. I had seen the Saliva Sisters play at Utah's International Jell-O Festival and they were simply outrageous! I called them. Over the phone, Adema Saliva (Rebecca Terry) told me the band simply didn't do weddings. I begged her to reconsider and when I mentioned that it was a surprise wedding there was a long and amused silence. "What do you mean, a surprise wedding?"

"The woman I am planning to marry has no idea I'm throwing a wedding."

"Are you serious?"

"Absolutely."

"Do you have any idea how crazy this sounds?"

"I do."

"That's just too crazy to pass up on something like that," replied Becky. "We'll do it!"

"By the way, do you, by any chance, do the Dixie Cups version of 'Chapel of Love'?"

"Absolutely!"

To be on the safe side, I sent out no invitations. I invited only the people whom I thought Alana would like to have at the wedding. There would be no distant cousins twice removed and none of the obligatory relatives from either side of the family. This was a wedding for Alana.

To provide cover for myself in the evening so I could make all the arrangements and contact people by phone and invite them to the wedding, I enrolled in a fly-tying course at Granite District's continuing education classes. I only attended the class one time and bought fishing flies that I passed off as my own patterns.

A good friend offered to fly me to a nearby state where we could buy booze at discount prices. I had thirsty friends. We landed in a brutal snowstorm and found ourselves without transportation to town. In a serious negotiation with the bearded man who ran the tower, we managed to borrow a beat-up pickup truck without the front windshield in exchange for a case of Moosehead beer. By the time we arrived in town, we were drenched and frozen. I arrived back home only minutes before Alana returned from work.

After considerable prodding, Alana's younger sister agreed to pose as Alana and go with me to secure the marriage license. I'd nicked all of Alana's personal information out of her wallet: driver's license, credit cards, and a social security card. In essence, I'd stolen her identity.

Together we rehearsed our script: When were you born? What is your height, weight, home address, social security number . . . anything that might trip us up.

On the day we went for the marriage license, her sister had done her hair just like Alana. We held hands, filled out the appropriate state forms, attended a Mickey Mouse lecture for prospective newly-weds taught by a sweaty little man with bad teeth. Upon completion we were given a small goody bag containing things one might need moving into a house: soaps, toothpaste, and other helpful items. There were, of course, no mini-bottles of champagne or condoms.

Time accelerated. I checked and double-checked the plans. Arrangements had been made for out-of-town guests to stay at condos in Deer Valley. Everybody who was invited accepted. This worried me. I wondered if, in the final days, somehow, somebody might spill the beans. I watched Alana carefully to see if she had the slightest hint of a surprise wedding. She didn't. In fact, we began discussing the possibility of getting married.

At one point, we actually made up a list of people we would like to have at the wedding. It was almost identical to the people sequestered away in safe houses waiting for the event. A couple of times, Alana would ask me for the list, planning to add or delete a name, and I wouldn't be able to find it. To her, I seemed distracted and uncertain about getting married.

"With my new job, I'm going to be traveling a great deal during April and May. June will get here sooner than you think, Jeff."

I wanted to say, *June will be here in 10 days.*

"You know it takes a great deal of effort to organize a wedding, Jeff. If you feel uncomfortable about June, we probably should talk about it before we get too far into the planning stage."

I wanted to tell her in the worst way. More than anything I wanted to say, *Yes! It does take a lot of work!* I wanted to tell her, to ask her then and there if she'd marry me. I wanted to tip her off just in case her girlfriends were correct and I was robbing her of planning her own wedding. But I didn't.

The week before the wedding Alana and I were having dinner with her parents. In casual conversation, I asked them if they were planning any winter trips. I hadn't told them of the surprise wedding because I knew there would be some serious concerns. Frankly, I didn't want them to know until the very last moment. I panicked when they mentioned they were headed to Palm Springs to watch the Bob Hope Classic on the same weekend I'd planned the wedding. I'd have to talk with them soon.

That night I dreamt I'd gone over to Alana's parents to talk with them about the wedding. In the dream, I'd asked her mother what has three hundred feet and yells, "SURPRISE!" Her mother stared blankly at me. "I don't know," she replied. "What has three hundred feet and yells, 'SURPRISE'?"

"Your daughter's surprise wedding," I blurted out.

"But I don't get it," she replied.

"I know. That's why I'm here. I'm going to marry your daughter on the twenty-eighth of January and I'd like you both to be at the wedding."

"But, Alana didn't say anything to us," she said, dejectedly. The color drained from her face. "How could you do something like that? My husband will want to counsel Alana. This is not right. She should have said something to us."

This was an uncomfortable dream. I explained to her that I'd spent three months planning out every detail of the wedding, and I wasn't about to have them spoil the occasion by trying to counsel Alana. I apologized for what appeared to be my lack of consideration but this was about their daughter's wedding and not about them. It was not a pretty dream.

Two days later, I drove over to their house and began with the punch line, "What has three hundred feet and yells 'SURPRISE!'" I had the strange feeling I already knew how this was going to turn out. It was awkward and confusing. I liked the dream better.

Four days before the wedding, guests began arriving from all over the country. I was driving back and forth from the Salt Lake International Airport to Park City. I continued to come home later and later every night. The event was gaining momentum. Alana finally cornered me and asked me what was wrong. My behavior had become . . . oh, slightly erratic.

"Jeff, are you seeing somebody else?" After all, I was leaving early in the morning and returning late at night and I smelled like I'd been drinking. I didn't try to justify my actions because I was terrified that I would spill my guts. "Talk to me Jeff. If you don't feel comfortable about getting married in June, or getting married period, I need to know this." She paused, looked directly into my eyes, and said, "This just isn't like you, Jeff. Whatever is going on, tell me, please. I'd rather know."

The pressure was unbearable and I felt guilty, but if I told her anything I would tell her everything. I'd gone this far and our friends were fantastic about keeping the secret so I remained silent.

The morning of the wedding I made Eggs Benedict, coffee, fresh orange juice, and served breakfast in bed to Alana. She was thumbing through a bride's magazine looking at wedding dresses. I flinched. "You know," she said, "there's not a single dress here that I like. They're either too much or too little." I sat next to her while she showed me the photographs.

"When you get married, what do you think you'd like to wear?" I asked.

"I don't know," she replied, "probably an elegant cocktail dress like the one you bought me for tonight's dinner."

It snowed all day. Around 5:30 p.m., an hour and a half before the ceremony, Alana wondered out loud, "Do you think Bill and Linda would mind if we postponed dinner at the Mariposa and just tucked in for the night?"

"With it snowing like this, they'd probably understand," I replied, trying not to overreact. "I'll give him a call."

Before I could pick up the phone, Alana said, "You know what, that's not right. Let's just go. It'll be good to see them."

"Okay."

I don't remember much about the drive to Silver Lake Lodge. Alana chatted about how beautiful the mountains looked dusted in snow. She talked a little about how she didn't want to have one of those weddings where the bride and groom didn't have a chance to enjoy the ceremony. Did I feel the same way?

"I can't think of any wedding where the bride seemed relaxed," Alana said, and then she asked me a series of questions: Had I thought anything about where we should get married? A church? Southern Utah? One of the ski resorts like Alta or Deer Valley? Maybe run off to San Francisco. Would I feel comfortable having Bill work with us on our wedding plans?

"I really haven't given it that much thought yet."

We met Bill at the front door of the Café Mariposa and were seated by the fireplace. Linda joined us and Bill and I excused ourselves to look at a private stock of wine. Bill informed me that 150 people were upstairs in the recently constructed chapel and the Saliva Sisters were set up, the banquet was prepared, and the justice of the peace was being served some wine, but we had one problem. How would we get Alana out of the restaurant and upstairs without raising suspicion? That had been the one flaw in my plan. I had no idea.

Returning to the table, Alana ordered a glass of Pinot Noir. Bill, Linda, and I ordered double martinis. Franklin, the executive chef, came out and visited the table, explaining the menu he had created especially for us. Of course, three out of the four of us knew the food would never arrive.

While we were having our cocktails Alana asked Bill if the resort ever did weddings. She mentioned we were interested in getting married in June and we'd like to have him help us plan the wedding. Although the lodge was usually closed during the summer, would it be possible to do something outside on one of the decks?

Simultaneously, three martinis were drained. Bill explained that the resort did, in fact, cater weddings. Were we interested in getting married in Salt Lake? Coming up to Deer Valley for a reception? He explained that Deer Valley was preparing for a wedding that very night and we could take a look at how things were set up before the guests arrived.

Bill escorted us through the long hall where a splendid buffet was set up in a dining area. Alana looked at the bar area and commented, "These people look like they are in for a good party." As we passed the buffet, I reached out and grabbed a small piece of beef and plopped it into my mouth. Alana slapped my hand, "This isn't your wedding. What do you think you're doing, paying for it?" I wanted to scream, "Yes, Alana, in more ways than you'll ever know." I looked up at the loft and could see heads bent in silence. There wasn't a sound. One hundred and fifty people were holding their breath at the top of the stairs and I was twenty-two steps away from asking Alana to marry me. I rehearsed my proposal lines carefully. The words were beginning to get mixed up. I was starting to get light-headed. When we reached the top of the stairs and Alana turned the corner into the chapel area, the Saliva Sisters broke into "The Chapel of Love" and I forgot everything I'd planned on saying to her.

Alana's Point of View

When I turned the corner, I stepped back because there was a wedding going on. A man turned to me with a video camera on his shoulder and said, "Smile for the camera man." I knew him. It was my brother Steve. I looked around. I began to recognize people that we knew. People who shouldn't be at Deer Valley because they didn't live here. The next thing I knew, our friend Lyn Felton ran up and slipped a garter around my leg, his wife, Norin, handed me a bouquet of flowers, and I turned around to Jeff, trying to make sense of this and he mumbled something. He's never at a loss for words and I didn't understand what he said. It still hadn't connected yet. Everything happened so fast.

"Alana, will you marry me?"

I thought he was joking and I started to laugh. "Alana, would you marry me and be my wife?" Then he added, "Are you in, or are you out?" I couldn't stop laughing. He looked so nervous. When I said, "Yes, and I wouldn't miss this for the world!" the crowd erupted. It sounded as though we were at the Super Bowl. People went wild. It was the most wonderful night I think I've ever had in my life. In every picture we are laughing and smiling. Together, we danced down the aisle and the rest, as we say, has been magic.

The Burn

It's like this: I'm sixty-two years old, a few pounds overweight, an occasional smoker, and I'm in need of some help. In all probability, I've got more years behind me than in front of me. In a moment of weakness, I find myself sitting alongside my wife talking to a body trainer at a new fitness center that has opened in the city. The "health associate" is a young man, trim, wrinkle free, and has muscles where I didn't even know muscles existed. When he speaks, I get the sense we are in this together and it makes me nervous. I'm tempted to ask him if I can light one up. And I'd do it in a heartbeat but I gave up smoking years ago. I'm trying to stay alive. This is why I'm here.

We fill out forms. The basics: name, height, weight, types of physical activity, and whether we have any limitations with regard to any of the workout equipment. This is where it gets tricky. I've seen the workout apparatus and it would make the Marquis de Sade envious. I look over to see what my wife has written down and when she notices she covers up her answers. Thanks. Thanks a lot. So I scribble "not to my knowledge."

My physical activity box looks kind of sparse so I whisper to my wife, "Do you think having sex counts as a physical activity?" and without missing a beat she replies, "Not in your case." Cute, but not funny.

Question number 10 asks: On a scale of 1 to 10, with 10 being the most serious, how committed are you about your workout goals? This is a tough one. I lie. I circle 9. After collecting our personal surveys, Mr. I-Got-Muscles-Between-My-Toes reviews them. I know he actually reads them because I watch his lips as he sounds out the big words. He asks my wife a few questions, makes some suggestions of classes that might be of interest to her. It's good stuff, the soft sell. When he gets to my application, he hesitates for a moment. His eyebrow muscles twitch. I get that uneasy feeling, like when I used to lie to my parents about thinning down their booze with water. We both know what's going on here.

"You're serious about working out. That's good."

He knows that I am lying. I blurt out, "I'm a 7."

"Pardon me?"

"I lied. I'm not a 9." The confession feels good. "I'm more of a 7, but I actually could be an 8."

He just looks at me.

"I am a 7!" I feel like this is the first night of a twelve-step program. "Hi, my name is Jeff and I'm a 7."

"So, do you want me to put down a 7?"

"Yes. I'm a 7."

I half expect him to say, "Is that your final answer?"

The Rookie (Journal Entry #1)

5:00 a.m. Today I begin my first workout. I'm a bit nervous.

8:00 a.m. I'm in way over my head. I showed up wearing high-top red Chuck Taylor Converse sneakers, some baggy shorts, and an old fishing T-shirt. I enrolled in a one-hour spin cycle class. The instructor said, and I think he did so for my benefit, "Just a few reminders. We'll all work at our own speed. It doesn't matter whether you are a first timer or not, this is all about having fun." My classmates wore spandex biking shorts, fancy magnetic clip-on biking shoes, biking gloves, and placed their water bottles into the holders on the frame. Two guys were actually wearing biking helmets. Seriously, what was that about?

I hung out on the back row of spinning bikes where people wouldn't hear me wheezing. A quarter of the way through the routine, our instructor had us turn up the tension on our bikes in order to prepare for an imaginary hill climb. Funky music floated out through a surround-sound system. The instructor had a space-age headset thingy on his head and talked to us. "Close your eyes. Imagine a place. A place to go that you love. A place that gives you pleasure." This was virtual imagery stuff. I was in the game. I visualized my favorite restaurant, La Champagne in Seattle, just up from Pike's Market. It's a wonderful French bistro. I peddled. I ordered Country Pate with toast points, a nice Chardonnay (not too oaky) and frog's legs. More wine. An assorted cheese plate with fruit. Some fine Port wine. Perhaps a dessert menu. I was out there in my own world.

"Sir?"

"What?"

The instructor startled me. He'd come out of his toe clips and descended from the elevated platform where he rode his bike to see how I was doing. He was standing next to me with the headphone thingy on so all the class could hear and they were staring at me.

"Are you all right?"

"Yes. Yes, I'm fine."

"You stopped peddling. And you were beginning to drool. I thought you were having a stroke."

"No, really . . . I'm fine. I was thinking about dessert."

"I see." He nodded, but I could tell he did not see.

I wanted to say, "I don't think so because La Champagne doesn't serve freaking tofu or veggie garden burgers or pretend food. Everything here is cooked in butter and olive oil with wine and cream sauces. Like it should be!" But I didn't.

9:00 a.m. I survived my first spin class. I was drenched in sweat and my legs felt wobbly. Walking out of the spinning room, a hard-bodied, attractive, thirty-something woman who didn't have an ounce of fat on her said, "Did you feel the *burn*?" I didn't know how to answer this because I definitely felt something. So I simply replied, "Yes, yes I felt the burn."

"It's cool, isn't it?"

"My *burn* feels hot," I replied.

"Hot? Well that's cool, too."

I was getting tripped up on the language of working out so I stopped while I was ahead.

What I felt was not the *burn*. It was the *chafe*. I felt *the chafe*. By 9:20 a.m. I was back home, lying stark naked on my back, my legs spread eagle with about an inch of baby powder dusted all over my balls. (A mental note: Next spin class wear biking shorts. P.S. Maybe try something else.)

I had a couple of days before the next spin class so I poked around looking at the other body-conditioning classes. The Body Pump class promised to be the hottest trend in body shaping. *With the use of the adjustable weight bar, participants will involve themselves in a series of squats, presses, curls, etc. to add strength and variety to your workout routine.* It came with a further guarantee that the class was, *Absolutely—without a doubt—FUN!* No, not my kind of fun.

The Rear Attitude class was billed as *The solution to gravity— just for your behind. A 25-minute class instructed by Professional Trainers who have your bottom line in mind.* Having checked out a few of the bottoms myself, it's a class I could easily get behind.

I looked at the conditioning classes: the cardio class, TNT, Step/Step Interval, Pilates, Ab Development, and the Xtreme spinning class. That would be my next order of business because I was familiar with the concept. Plus, it promised, *A 60-minute killer and thriller of a class that might be the most fun you could have going nowhere!* And who was I if not a fun-seeking cyclist?

After the chafed crotch incident with Carl, I joined the Xtreme cycling class with Hans.

"Hi, my name is Hans and people call me Hans." Perhaps I had missed something here because I started laughing. It just seemed funny. "Hi, my name is Hans and people call me Hans." I understood this wasn't rocket science, but still . . .

As we began our flatland warm up, Hans asked us to introduce ourselves. There's Heidi, Chris, Steve, Mark, Talesha, Amber, Autumn, TJ, and Heather . . . the only thing missing are the Musketeer ears. "Hi, my name is Jeff, but I go by Kevin and the 'r' in my name is silent." At 6:00 a.m. this seemed pretty funny to me, but I was clearly in the minority. My first instructor had selected New Age music for his workout routine, but Hans preferred Megadeath and Metallica. He wore a World Wrestling Federation wife-beater shirt and was definitely in a different world than I was. After the workout, I was sopped in sweat but I had survived. It was euphoric and I wanted to break out my lighter, flame it, and scream, "I feel the burn! Hans! Hans, Megadeath Rules!"

Helga, the instructor in week number three of the cycling class, provided me with some of my greatest material. Weighing at most a buck twenty-five, she was the personification of a *valley* girl. Although I can't be certain, I think she crossed her multiple vitamins with some good cross-top speed. She was nonstop dribble, filling all potential of silence with a box full of clichés. "Okay, class, like this workout can be whatever you want it to be. Like, if it's cardio you want, or like if you want to go for stamina . . . go for like stamina. But whatever, it's all about fun. Fun is like what this is all about."

No, Helga, this is not like all about fun. For me, Helga, this is all about guilt and sweat.

"This weekend, like the weather was sooo great. I went on a bike ride with my dad. And like my dad is really tall and skinny but he has a gut like he's going to have a baby. Like from the back you could never tell he had a gut. So, I'm like worried about him keeping up with me but he like surprises me and I had a really hard time keeping up with him. Isn't that freaky? How you like you do that sometimes? It was really cool, you know, getting to work out with your own father and I'm thinking . . . even with the gut and being old, my father's almost forty-five, he's in pretty good shape. It was totally awesome! So, like I'm thinking, even if you're old like my dad you don't have to give up on life or anything. Just go with the flow."

Even at 6:10 this is deep. I'll keep this in mind. Maybe I'll get this tattooed on my forearm. In curlicue, it might say something. The "Even if you're old, you don't have to give up on life or anything" makes this important.

"This is like one of my favorite groups. . . . Smashing Pumpkins . . . so I'm just like going to let the music speak to us. The only command I'll give during this series of hill climbs will be to turn the tension up on the bike by a quarter of a turn each time. Remember, if you're tight with your bike, your bike will be tight with you. Okay? We're coming to the first hill. Up yours a quarter. Do it now. Feel the burn."

"UP YOURS!" I reply under my breath and the other fat guy next to me starts laughing.

"Right on," he whispers back to me and it sustains us for the remainder of the hour.

It's dodgy being a first-timer in one of these health clubs. Now that I've been around, it is easy to spot the pretenders—the first timers. They tend to walk about tentatively, staring at the machines, looking over their shoulders, trying to suck in their stomachs and blend in. Stop it already. It's not necessary. There is a mathematical equation in health clubs that is absolute. For every ten people who are in better shape than you, there are ten people in worse shape.

But I can offer some advice for those people who don't want to look like rubes.

NEVER speak of complete body parts. Complex sentences do not belong in this environment. For example: If an instructor asks what part of your body you are planning to work on, never—and I mean never—say you are planning to work on your abdominal muscles. This is a dead giveaway. Simply say, *Abs. Quads. Pecs.*

Sprinkle any conversation with the word *reps*. Example: "I'm doing 5 sets of 10 reps for my abs." Even if you don't know what this means, it sounds good and people will nod in agreement. They know you know.

Keep a small spray bottle filled with water wrapped in your workout towel. When nobody is looking, squirt your face and T-shirt to make it look like you are deeply into a workout. This way people will keep their distance. You'll look like you are in the zone. Distance is a good thing.

Always leave the next person guessing. Say you are working on a weight machine to build up your *pecs* and you are doing three sets of 30 reps at 90 pounds. When you've completed your workout, and this is critical, make certain nobody is watching, then move the weight up to 180 pounds. Make a big fanfare of wiping your brow. Breathe heavily. Use some of the mist from your spray bottle if necessary. Take a moment and wipe down the machine and wait until somebody comes along to use the same machine. Tell them you're done and then move to a spot where you can spy on them. If they're amateurs, they'll sit down, strain to make *the lift* and be catapulted halfway across the weight room. This is as good as it gets. If they return to the machine, they'll move the weight peg to a manageable range of about 75 and marvel at the little bald-headed guy who did three sets of 30 *reps* at 180 pounds. It's awesome.

When working on a slant board to build up your *abs* in search of the perfect stomach *rip* and somebody plops down next to you, use creative mathematics. Be generous to yourself. Round up. Round up a great deal. Sit-up number 20 can easily become sit-up number 97. So, with three more, you're busting the 100 mark. And trust me on this, you'll start believing it and it feels good.

After six weeks I've settled into a serious routine. I've outlasted a number of the people who, like myself, took the oath to lose a little weight and get in shape. I have shed some weight and tightened up a bit. I'm down to one chin and can fit into slacks that I haven't seen in the front of the closet for a long time. It's a good thing for me. I needed it.

Most of all I've learned some things about myself. I'll never be a workout freak, a person who lives for *the burn*, a person whose life centers on daily workouts. Believe me, there are plenty of folks out there like that and I respect them for it. I'll leave spandex to those who look good in spandex. I'm at the gym because of history and cards. Both are important in life.

My father died young. He was the age I am now. After a lifetime of tobacco and alcohol abuse, there was nothing left of him. I remember his eyes the night I drove him to the hospital to die. They were milky and complicated. As we drove, his eyes sucked up the surrounding freeway lights, the fat February snowflakes as they floated lazily across the high beams of the car and out onto the Salt Lake Country Club golf course. I knew what he was thinking. He wasn't coming home again.

"When you get back from the hospital we'll have go get out on that course," I promised.

He struggled to speak. "Sure." He reached out and placed his hand on my forearm and squeezed. There was nothing to it. Skin and bones, translucent pale skin stretched loosely over a road map of veins. He nodded toward my mother in the back seat. I understood what the look meant.

"I will," I said. "I will."

Those eyes haunt me. They belonged to my father. They belonged to a man I knew very little about. A man who never balanced himself. A man who left a great number of important things unsaid in our family.

My daughter remembers very little about him. She kept a photograph of him pinned to a corkboard just over her desk for many years and then it disappeared. In the photograph, she is sitting next to my father at the dinner table and they are wearing red-checkered napkins on their heads. It was a wonderful photograph full of laughter. It is a fine memory. It's a good image to cling to.

My father never lived to see his grandson John or my sister's daughter Lisa. He would have enjoyed them. They are bright and funny adults now, but he never gave himself that chance.

My mother passed away ten years ago, puzzled and confused and shrunken by the horrors of Alzheimer's. She did not get to meet her great-grandson, my daughter's first child, Jack. He was named after my father.

My sister has battled with the aftershock of breast cancer and I have dealt with prostate cancer for over eight years and my only brother has disappeared to the jungles of Nicaragua and is seldom in touch with any of us. We all carry the weight of family.

So, in the end, I know why I roll out of a warm bed in the early morning and leave my wife sleeping quietly. I do it to give myself a chance, to stack the deck any way I can in my favor. I need more wind to fish the great trout runs. I want to be a better husband, a better father. I want to grow up with my children and their grandchildren. These are selfish reasons but they are real and they are mine. They run deeper than my own humor, something more than essence, something at once of me and beyond me. This is the burn I feel. This is my burn.

Death Row, Part 1

Christmas 1995 was closing in on the Valley High School newspaper staff, and for a group of truly remarkable students, the brainstorming sessions were anything but remarkable. *The Liberator* was an award-winning newspaper since its inception four years earlier when a student in my literature class, Scott Kerbin, had wondered out loud "Why don't we have a school newspaper like other schools?" I replied by telling him that we didn't have any facilities or equipment, we dealt with a district that expressed little interest in supporting "at risk" students, there was no money in the budget, and none of the teachers had any free time to teach the class. He just looked at me and said, "So, that's never stopped us before."

When I brought up Scott's comments in a faculty meeting, there was tremendous excitement and support for the project. I agreed to run a newspaper during my lunch hour two days a week.

Scott placed posters around the school inviting potential journalists to come in and interview with us during lunch hour. The faculty talked to students about the importance, particularly in a school like Valley, of making certain that "our" voices were being heard. Slowly, we began to muster up some interest and soon we had a core group of about twelve students interested in writing for the paper. Not a single student, in the first year of our paper, had any journalism experience. But, because they were hungry and because they were hungry to tell stories about their lives and the lives of their fellow students, *The Liberator* staff produced some pretty hard-hitting articles in its first year of existence. These articles were not the standard fare for high school newspapers in an extremely conservative school district.

There were no articles about team sports, prom royalty, or favorite teachers because we didn't have any athletic teams or proms, and the faculty wanted to stay out of the paper. We all knew what we did and why we loved teaching at the school. That was enough. Instead, the staff wrote articles that meant something to the populace. Editions of *The Liberator* included stories about child abuse, dangerous new street drugs, teen suicide, and domestic violence. It was hard journalism and it drew the attention of other schools and, unfortunately, the superintendent of our school district. Almost without exception, following the printing of an edition of *The Liberator*, I found myself either being called to the district office to discuss the content of the paper or, more conveniently, I might just find myself on the end of a phone call from one of the junior members of the district hierarchy warning me about the negative reaction from the community due to our publication. I finally stopped responding to all summons and phone calls and, eventually, when our newspaper began to receive prestigious journalism awards, we were left alone.

Admittedly, I was getting a bit agitated with the staff with three weeks left before the Christmas holiday break. Our Christmas issue was at the printer, a press owned by the parents of one of our students. His company printed the paper without cost to us because two of his children had attended and graduated from Valley and believed the school and faculty had saved his children's lives.

"I'm not seeing anything on the idea board that would interest me."

"Jesus, Metcalf, we just put the paper to bed!" Andrea remarked.

"True. But we have a deadline when we get back and nothing moves me yet."

I walked to the coffee pot, poured a cup of stale coffee, and sat back down at the circle of desks. When the silence became almost unbearable, one of the most unlikely of students, Josh, spoke up. By nature Josh was quiet but this year, after a horrific accident that severely scarred his face, he was much more withdrawn. Josh was lucky to be alive and we were all glad to have him back in class.

"What if we did an article on the guy that the state is going to execute by firing squad?" he suggested quietly.

"John Albert Taylor?" offered another staff member.

"Yes."

"What sort of article do you envision?" I asked him.

"Maybe an interview about why he murdered that little girl."

"That won't happen. He's claimed he was innocent."

"Plus, he's refused every single interview request with any newspapers or networks."

"Why?"

"He wants to embarrass the State of Utah."

"That's not hard to do." The class laughed.

"Apparently Geraldo Rivera's show offered Taylor fifty thousand dollars for an exclusive interview and he told them to go fuck themselves."

"So, why would he want to talk to us?"

"I don't know," Josh quietly replied, "maybe he could identify with us in some way."

Josh's comments sobered the class. The idea, on many levels, that we had something in common with a murderer seemed, on the surface, fairly ludicrous. But as I surveyed the faces in the room, there were shadows and guarded narratives that had been stashed so deeply in the bones that they could not be spoken of yet. I knew many of the students' stories personally and several of these students had led harsh lives. I suspect it had a great deal to do with why the newspaper staff made such tough journalists. They wrote about things they knew and many of those stories were not pretty.

"Josh, how would you go about contacting him?" I asked.

"I'd write him a letter asking him for an interview."

"I'll help you with the letter," Lindsey offered from the other side of the room. Lindsey's personality was the exact polar opposite of Josh's. She was energetic, humorous, tough, straightforward, and ready to "throw down" if she felt it necessary and could absolutely disarm you moments later with her charm.

"Get me a draft of the letter by the end of the period," I said, and they collected their journals and headed to the back of the room and began a draft while the rest of us plugged along on the brainstorming session.

Clearly, the staff that first laughed at the idea began to realize that if, and this was a long-shot, Josh and Lindsey managed to wrangle an interview, it would be the largest single story to come out of the State of Utah in decades, and it would draw major international media attention. This would be the state's last sanctioned firing squad and John Albert Taylor had been very clear that he wanted to make his execution a public humiliation for the State of Utah.

The first draft of the letter was horrible. It offered nothing compelling, nothing of the curiosity that I suspected was necessary to get Mr. Taylor's attention. It did not speak to who we were at this school and all the obstacles these students had overcome in their lives. Valley High School was an alternative high school for students who did not fit into traditional high schools. All the students who entered Valley did so of their own accord. It was, and still remains to this day, a place of magic with humanistic curricula built on the foundation of the humanities.

Josh and Lindsey were writing to a man who had refused all interviews to date. They were writing to a man who, in less than two months, would be strapped into a chair with a hood placed over his head, a target pinned directly over his heart, and executed by firing squad. If the executioners were accurate, four .30-caliber bullets would blow the back of his chest out and he would be dead. Taylor had rejected the option of lethal injection in favor of the firing squad because he didn't want to be "flopping around" on a table and he wanted to create a media circus around his death.

The second letter was not much better, but on the third draft Josh and Lindsey made a compelling case that did not request an interview but instead asked John Taylor about his own journey through life and school. Together they framed a series of questions that they believed might get a response from Mr. Taylor. That afternoon, I stuck the letter in the mail.

"Do you think we'll hear from him?" Lindsey asked.

"I really don't know. But you and Josh gave yourself a chance. You asked."

A week later, without response from John Albert Taylor, we went on Christmas break. It was a long shot and I wasn't expecting Josh or Lindsey to hear anything from John Albert Taylor.

Wednesday, January 3, 1996

As was my custom, I arrived early to school following the Christmas break. My first class wasn't until noon. I visited with the office staff, headed to the faculty room to put a pot of coffee on, grabbed all my holiday mail, and walked down the hall to my classroom. Once inside, I sifted through the mail. There was nothing from the Utah State Penitentiary. Nothing at all. I hadn't expected a response. With the media circus this was becoming, how could we expect the letter even made it into John Albert Taylor's hands? Josh and Lindsey's letter, at best, would have been in a stack of the thousand letters a day Taylor would receive requesting interviews or offering prayers for a stay of execution, hate mail, and fan mail from all over the world.

Monday, January 8, 1996

Absolutely nothing. *The Liberator* staff was moping along feeling that this great idea for an interview was disappearing. Logically, when we tried to separate our disappointment with the reality of the facts, the thought of actually procuring a personal interview on Death Row was preposterous. Add to the equation the simple fact that Taylor would be executed in just eighteen days, it seemed well reasoned that he might have more pressing issues in front of him than an interview by a couple of high school journalists. At the end of class, Lindsey walked up to me and said, "I know we're going to get an interview. I had a dream that we got to go onto Death Row. Weird, huh?"

"It sounds more like a nightmare," I replied, jokingly.

"It'll happen. Just wait."

Monday, January 15, 1996

In the staff meeting Taylor's name wasn't mentioned for the first time since we'd discussed him before the break. Hope for an interview had vanished and we explored the question of doing a pro/con article about capital punishment. The execution was taking place in our own backyard and every night the news was flooded with sound bites of people in favor of the death penalty, those opposed to it, Amnesty International, various churches holding prayer vigils, and those of the lunatic fringe wearing signs volunteering to be part of the firing squad. National and international press had essentially created a siege around the Point of the Mountain (Utah State Prison).

"Hey, Metcalf," Lindsey called over her shoulder, "don't give up. He'll write. I know it."

I nodded my head.

Wednesday, January 17, 1996

On the way back to my office, I thumbed through my mail and was stunned to discover a letter from inmate #19789, housing unit 21-2305, occupant John Taylor, mailed on January 14 and addressed to *The Liberator*, Valley High School, Sandy, Utah. Most curious to me was that the letter had been opened. It would have happened at the district office or, more disturbingly, in our own office. I read the letter from John Albert Taylor. It was six pages written in longhand on yellow legal-pad paper. He answered every question Josh and Lindsey asked. At the end, he'd requested that, if possible, he'd like to be interviewed by them personally. He would grant them the only interview before his execution.

I couldn't help but think of Lindsey's dream and her unwavering belief that Taylor would respond to us. This was a story any journalist in their right mind would die for, so why us? I immediately became suspicious of Taylor and his motives. What was the angle? Was it one more chance to rub the world's faces in all of this by granting the only interview to a couple of high school journalists? It would not be out of character for him. I read and reread the letter several times looking for a clue, a motive behind his request. Did the letter truly "impress" him as he had written in his salutation?

1/14/96 (Word for word transcription)

Dear Mr. Anderson and Ms. Stevenson,

    I was very impressed with your letter and amazed at the depth of your questions. I appreciate the opportunity you have given me to express my thoughts.

    I have several reasons for answering your questions when I have continuously refused others, but the primary reason is the hope that something I have to say may prevent one, or more, of your fellow students from further ruining their young lives as I have.

        I strongly believe in life after death,
an eternal life. I am being baptized
Catholic on the 16th of January.
        I chose the firing squad because a
murder is about to take place, regardless
of my sentence, a life, my life, is going
to be violently ripped away from me, and
the firing squad demonstrates that fact.
Also it makes people aware that the act is
an intentional one, not some quiet peaceful
accident. Because I am not guilty of the
charge I was convicted of. So I want it
shown that I was callously & brutally
murdered. Lastly, there have been cases
where, during lethal injection, the victim
became conscious and were therefore forced
a sentient being to their own death.

The letter continued for five more pages and was, in many
regards, an effort on Taylor's part to voice his innocence in the
murder of Charla King. Did Taylor truly see himself, to some
small degree, in the stories of Josh and Lindsey? Perhaps this
was a last-minute act of kindness or generosity on Taylor's part?
It was too easy. What wasn't I seeing? What did I know about
John Albert Taylor? Cold facts: He raped his own sister when she
was twelve years old. In 1989 John Albert Taylor was convicted
of the rape and murder of eleven-year-old Charla Nicole King.
Taylor raped and then strangled her to death with a telephone
cord. This offer of an interview was not motivated by an act of
kindness. I was certain of this.

Midway through the morning a dark thought crossed my
mind. Lindsey would be Charla King's exact age had she lived.
Taylor had spent most of his prison life in solitary confinement.

Inside the penitentiary, there is an unspoken code of unacceptable crimes. Child rape and then murder top the list. Because of the nature of his crime and conviction, Taylor's life expectancy in a maximum-security population would be brief. It wasn't a leap to imagine Taylor's request for a personal interview was nothing more than an attempt to get "close" to some young adults. I was convinced his agreement to allow this interview was completely voyeuristic on Taylor's part. I was beginning to have second thoughts about the interview. A part of me considered wadding up the letter and throwing it in the trash. No harm, no foul, but I was unsettled enough by the notion that I decided to drop by the principal's office to talk through this with him.

Our principal at the time was Clyde Mellberg, a decent man who, for the most part, allowed a very dedicated faculty to run the school. To some degree, visiting him was part of a careful protocol we all followed. As a faculty, we pushed the district boundaries on a daily basis. As long as Principal Mellberg knew what we were doing before we did it, he was supportive of almost anything the faculty initiated. I did a quick knock on his door and stepped into his office. I wasn't prepared for the exchange we had.

"Just what the hell do you think you're doing, Metcalf?"

"How about we start with a 'Happy New Year,' Mellberg?"

"Taking students onto Death Row? That'll never happen. Do you think the district office will give you permission?"

I was backpedaling because I wasn't expecting such an onslaught from Mellberg. How in God's name could he have known about this? I hadn't discussed this with a soul. Then it occurred to me.

"You opened my mail?"

"It wasn't addressed to anybody in particular," he replied quickly.

"It was addressed to *The Liberator*, for Christ's sake! You know that's a federal crime, don't you, Mellberg?"

"Why are you always pushing these kids so hard, Metcalf?"

"Punishable by up to ten years in a federal prison and up to a $250,000 fine."

"I'm not going to give you permission to take anybody from the newspaper staff onto Death Row and I can guarantee you the district office will back me up."

"Really? Do you think so?"

"I'd bet on it."

"You've got a deal. I'll bet they will. And when they do, we'll need a decent tape recorder. The one we use for interviews is a Sesame Street recorder. It's got Burt and Ernie on it."

"Not going to happen."

"I'll be taking those two students onto Death Row. District permission or not, this is an opportunity of a lifetime for them or any other journalist."

"Not when I'm done talking with the superintendent."

"Well, Mellberg, if you're so damn certain about this, call him. Call him while I'm standing right here."

"I just might."

"Then do it."

The minute I challenged him, I wished I hadn't. On a number of occasions, Mellberg and I had played poker against each other in Montana. He owned a great deal of property in West Yellowstone and whenever I headed north on a fly-fishing trip, I'd drop by his place, drink a bit, grab dinner or cook in his kitchen, and then, if we were inclined, we'd head to our favorite bar, play poker for a couple of hours, and then I'd often crash in his guest room. He was bluffing.

"Go ahead, pick up the phone." He did. When he got the superintendent on the line, I sat down across the desk from him. I listened carefully as he told his own version of the narrative which was truly scattered. Had cooler heads prevailed we might have at least chatted about the situation but we were both rather hotheaded and as much as we did like each other, we'd busted heads on numerous occasions. It didn't sound very good from my seat. I had a couple of staunch supporters at the district office but the odds of having one of them on the line were not in my favor. Neither of us would look good in the moment. The first day of a new year and you had a couple of faculty nagging at you already. It was stupid and we both knew better. Mellberg was on the phone with the superintendent and I wasn't. There was a sudden and somber shift in Mellberg's face. He stopped talking and listened.

"Yes . . . I know he is, but," and something spoken on the other end stopped him. "He didn't say." Another pause. "Because I opened up a letter from the Utah State Prison and read it myself. That's how I knew."

There are many moments in my life where I have spoken up in my professional and personal life without thinking about the repercussions. In a number of instances I wish I could go back and replay the tape. This was one of these moments. I recognized that look on Mellberg's face. He'd backed himself into a corner by admitting to the superintendent that he'd violated a federal law by opening up our mail. Mellberg swiveled in his chair so his back was toward me.

"No, it wasn't," he shifted uncomfortably. "The newspaper staff." A long pause followed by, "I know it is. Uh-huh, uh-huh . . . yes, I will, I'll tell him." Mellberg hung up and turned back toward me.

"Well?"

"You can do the interview if you get access into the prison. The parents will have to sign a release of liability form and the district will take no responsibility if anything goes wrong."

"That's great," I said. "Thanks for calling."

"Don't press your luck, Metcalf."

This was awkward and it wasn't the way we worked together. I'd known Mellberg since my first year of teaching and I liked him a great deal. I just about opened my mouth to apologize, when he said, "Is there anything else you want to say, Metcalf?"

"Yes. I'll need a purchase order for the new tape recorder. We'll need it when we go onto Death Row." I turned and headed back to my classroom. Whether or not I understood what we were about to do or how we would do it, *The Liberator* had two journalists who would have the only opportunity to interview a cold-blooded murderer before his execution. If they were interested in the challenge, the story was theirs and I'd do everything in my power to make it happen.

Death Row, Part 2

Josh and Lindsey were like little children when I told them John Albert Taylor had indeed written them back. I showed them the letter and allowed them each time to digest it. Finally, Lindsey asked the most obvious question, "Do you think we can get permission to go onto Death Row?"

"It depends, but there's a great deal working against us."

"Like what?" Josh asked.

"Permission from the director of Point of the Mountain. His name is Jack Ford and he's a no-nonsense sort of man. My sense is that he's in stress mode right now. Bringing a couple of high school journalists and their teacher onto Death Row is not on his priority list."

"What about Valley High and the district?" Josh asked.

"They're on board. They think it's a great idea," I said, feeling a bit strange muttering the words.

"Seriously?" Lindsey asked.

"For the most part."

"How are we going to do it?" asked Lindsey, sensing a great idea getting mired down in red tape, endless permission slips, and disappearing from the realm of possibility.

"We have to make it a priority for Jack Ford. He'll want to dismiss us because we're not the 'real' press. We can't let that happen.

The media circus has already begun. Start watching television, the local news. Supporters against capital punishment are standing vigil twenty-four hours a day outside the penitentiary. People are surrounding the prison in a candlelight vigil. Camera crews from all over the world have set up live broadcast hook-ups."

"Jesus," exhaled Josh, "I didn't think it would be that big a deal."

"And I'm going to need to talk to your parents about this."

"They'll be fine," they replied. "Why?"

"It'll get crazy and we need to be prepared. I need permission slips signed from them." Lindsey and Josh nodded. "It's going to be a circus. We can't say anything to anybody about the interview. At least not outside of the classroom. When we meet today we'll let them know Taylor wrote back but we've got to keep all this under wraps. If it gets out into the world, it'll be impossible for us to do our job. We'll be the freak show. Silence will be the key to the success of this. What do you think?"

They nodded in agreement. "But the biggest problem is that John Albert Taylor will be executed in less than ten days. We've got to work hard and fast. If we back off the printing time, we probably have a week to pull this all together."

That afternoon, we told the staff about Taylor's request for an interview. Then we began a very serious discussion about what our next seven days would look like. We still didn't have permission from the Department of Corrections. Jack Ford was the key to our success. If he didn't agree to the interview, it was over. He wouldn't have to say the words. The simplest way to dismiss us was to say we needed to petition the Prison Board and wait for an answer. It would be over. He could throw a series of bogus requirements in our way that would be impossible to complete before the execution. We faced the same possibility with our own school district. Suppose the district required a letter from us signed by the school board, the parents, and a psychologist who would attest to Josh and Lindsey's ability to handle such a dramatic event before allowing us to go onto Death Row.

My first job was to convince Jack Ford of the importance of the interview. Although I'd never personally met Mr. Ford, we had a number of friends in common and I wouldn't hesitate to drop a few names if need be. That afternoon I made an appointment with Mr. Ford for the next day.

Back in the class, we did what we did best. The staff broke the story down and gave assignments to the staff reporters. It was necessary to go to several public libraries and collect information dating back to the crime. We'd need court transcripts of the trial and scan the archives of our two local papers, the *Deseret News* and the *Salt Lake Tribune* for any unusual sidebars, names of neighbors, officers on duty, arresting officers, the arraignment, defense and prosecuting attorneys, and anybody remotely connected to the Charla King murder. And of course, if at all possible, we'd need to interview Charla's parents. Then the students of *The Liberator* staff got to work.

I will say this—many years after the event—the professionalism of the students on the staff would rival any current news organization past or present. They collected snippets of interviews, began to reconstruct the events of the murder, tracked down phone numbers, and collected valuable information for us to begin to understand a timeline of events and try, if at all possible, to gain any insight into John Albert Taylor. They worked before and after school. On a couple of nights we'd order pizza and work until the early morning hours. There was a palpable sense of urgency. Taylor had waived his appeals and we had less than ten days to compile the data, read and become familiar with the transcripts, and then do a trial run having Josh and Lindsey interview me as John Albert Taylor.

Wednesday, January 17

My meeting with Jack Ford was brief and to the point. Although he wasn't in support of the idea of the interview, he believed that

Taylor had the right to be interviewed, even if it was to a couple of high school reporters.

"You know," he said, "Taylor's been asked by almost every newspaper and television agency in the world for an interview and he's turned them all down. Why do you think he agreed to an interview now? And with your students?"

"It's an interesting question, isn't it?" I replied.

"Wait until the press hears he's granted a couple of high school students the only interview. The media will overrun your school and those kids' lives will never be the same. It's been a circus around here."

"We don't plan to tell anybody about the interview for that very reason."

"Then what's the point?"

"We'll print the copy of our newspaper a couple of days before the execution. It'll be an exclusive story and the students of Valley High will be the first to read about it."

"Seriously?"

"Yes, and I'd like to ask you not to let anyone know about this. These students are minors and they have a right to their privacy."

Ford looked perplexed but agreed to the request. In turn, he required that I be in the interview with Josh and Lindsey. Additionally, he wanted to film the interview for the prison archives. It was a fair exchange. We would be picked up on the twenty-third in an unmarked Department of Corrections vehicle and brought into the prison. Once inside, we'd be searched and escorted onto Death Row. We'd be held in holding and then taken to an interview room where there would be four chairs. Each of us would have a chair and there would be a long rectangular table separating us from John Albert Taylor.

"Will there be a guard in the room?" I asked, talking through the worst-case scenario I could imagine.

"There will be one just outside the door." Ford read my mind, "You'll be safe."

That afternoon in class, I pulled Josh and Lindsey aside and explained the situation to them, asking them if they still felt comfortable about going into prison and interviewing Taylor. I had my own concerns, wondering to some degree if Clyde Mellberg wasn't right, that maybe in fact I did push my students too hard.

"At any time before the interview, when we arrive at the prison, or even before we get onto Death Row . . . if you want to pull out, we can."

"Why would we want to do that?" Lindsey asked. "This is a big story and we'll be ready."

January 18, 19, and 20

Thursday, Friday, and Saturday were a whirlwind of energy. Josh and Lindsey prepared for their first attempt at an interview with John Albert Taylor on Sunday at our home. Neither of the students knew I'd be playing John Albert Taylor and that my wife, Alana, and I had set up our dining room area to look as much like a prison as possible. I'd worked with Josh and Lindsey for two years so the idea that I'd be playing Taylor would be funny to them. My job was to make certain that didn't happen.

When they arrived at our house, I was nowhere to be found. My wife escorted them to our dining room and placed them at the table and told them Mr. Taylor would be in shortly for the interview. She said nothing else to them and disappeared to our office in the basement where I was in slippers, gray medical scrubs and a bathrobe. My hands were locked in a pair of handcuffs we'd purchased for a Halloween costume.

"Okay," my wife said, "you look scary enough. Where's the belt to your robe?"

"We don't get belts on the inside. Afraid we'll hang ourselves."

"Okay, now you're making me nervous. Do you think this is such a good idea?"

"Take me to the interview now!"

My wife brought me into the dining room and seated me directly across from Josh and Lindsey and then disappeared. However, before she did, she looked at the students and said, "If, at any time you feel in danger, call for me and I'll get you out of here."

They started to smile like they'd figured out the game we were playing, but they had no idea what was coming next. Neither did I.

Lindsey started laughing and Josh smiled. "My God, Metcalf . . . you really look like you're a . . ."

"You think something is funny about all this?" I yelled. "I don't know who Metcalf is, but if you think this is a game, we're done here."

"Hey, man, Lindsey was just . . ."

"Don't 'Hey, man' me, kid. And she don't look like she needs help from the likes of you."

Lindsey quickly jumped in to defend Josh. "Metcalf, there's no need to be like this, we get it. We can do the interview without . . ."

"Guard! Guard! Get me out of here! This interview is over."

I stood up and when my wife arrived to escort me out of the room, Lindsey stopped her.

"Mr. Taylor," she said, "I apologize for our behavior. We're just a bit nervous with all of this."

Josh overlapped Lindsey, "Thank you for responding to our letter. We feel very honored that you chose us for the interview. May we record this interview?"

"Yes," I said and sat down for a two-hour interview in which I never backed down in my role as John Albert Taylor and they never shied away from tough questions and, more importantly, the follow-up questions.

"Interview is over, Mr. Taylor needs to be escorted back to his cell." My wife then helped me up out of the chair and took me out of the dining room. When she returned to the kitchen, which adjoined the dining room, she asked Josh and Lindsey if they wanted coffee or anything.

"Coffee for me, please," Lindsey said, "with a little milk and sugar."

"Me, too, please," echoed Josh.

"You have a beautiful house," Lindsey remarked.

"Thanks," Alana replied and sipped coffee with them.

Finally, Lindsey asked the obvious, "Where's Metcalf? Isn't he coming back in to talk with us?"

"He's not here," she replied, adding, "he plays tennis every Sunday and doesn't get home until around noon." And then, just to mess them up more, she asked, "Was he expecting you?"

I could see both students from my position in the hallway. The moment had become truly awkward and I almost stepped in to break the tension, to tell them they'd done a wonderful job with the interview and that they'd do a fantastic job when we got onto Death Row, but I slid back into my room and waited until they excused themselves and left the house. When I'd changed out of my robe and scrubs and went in the kitchen for a cup of coffee, Alana spoke.

"That was cruel. I think you went too far."

Maybe I did go too far but my instincts told me to get these two high school reporters ready for whatever might happen on Death Row. I was worried—not only for their safety but also for their ability to be prepared for anything that Taylor might throw at them. Our interview was on January 23 and Taylor was being executed three days later. What did he have to lose?

"The truth is, Alana, I probably wasn't hard enough on them."

January 22

The upcoming interview was pushing us all in ways we never expected. The class was under a great deal of pressure. When I saw Josh and Lindsey in class, they didn't speak to me. I asked them if they were ready for the interview, giving them an opening to maybe say something like, "Screw you, Metcalf!" or at the least say something like, "That was a little overboard and we didn't like you treating us like we were stupid." Anything. I could have taken anything. Just throw me some sort of bone so I could apologize and let them know how fantastically well they did in the mock interview, how they held their composure when I'd lost mine, how brave they were, and how much I respected them and every single student in the class, but they offered me nothing. It was important for them to keep this thick skin on for the real interview.

When our class ended, I kept them back for a few minutes to remind them that we were interviewing a condemned man. What could happen in the interview might be uncomfortable and could get out of hand. If that was the case, we could be out of the interview room in seconds. All they needed to give me was the sign.

What John Albert Taylor did to Charla King was horrific. The damage he caused to her family, her neighbors, and to the community was reprehensible, beyond any sort of rationale . . . anything a sane person can comprehend. But, I insisted, "We need to treat him with courtesy and leave our emotions at the gate. You are journalists, so do your job."

"We will," they said in unison.

"I'll see you tomorrow."

January 23 (The Interview)

I couldn't sleep much the night before the interview. My stomach was churning and the little sleep I managed to snatch was layered in horrific images in a series of slow-motion nightmares. A prison break. Death Row inmates breaking loose while we were interviewing John Albert Taylor and Taylor having orchestrated all of it. In one such moment I remember looking at him like he might actually help us or say something to the other convicts to keep them at arms' length from Josh and Lindsey; instead he rose from his chair, plucked the chain shackles out of the wall like they were nothing at all, and unclasped his handcuffs with a bobby pin he'd stashed under his tongue. Then he started laughing at us.

It was 3:34 a.m. and I wasn't getting back to sleep so I bundled up, grabbed our dog, Patch, and headed out of the house for a walk. It was beginning to snow lightly and the forecast called for heavy storm warnings during the remainder of the week. I had some serious concerns about what we were about to do.

As per our arrangement with Jack Ford, an unmarked state car picked us up at Valley High School mid-morning. The driver was a corrections officer for the prison. There was little conversation during the ride. He carefully explained what would happen when we arrived at the prison. We'd meet Jack Ford. From his office we'd be escorted to a room where we would be searched for any contraband items and we would be required, at least Josh and I would be required, to remove our belts before entering Death Row. A female corrections officer in a separate room would search Lindsey. Then we'd meet together and be escorted onto Death Row. Once on Death Row, we were instructed not to look toward the left where the inmates were housed because "any number of perverted things could happen." We would be escorted to the second visiting room where we would wait until John Albert Taylor was brought in for the interview.

The atmosphere surrounding the prison was more serene than I expected. It was snowing fat, wet flakes. The cameras and television vans with satellite hook-ups covered in snow looked like prehistoric dinosaurs. The tension we'd all witnessed on nightly news, the shouting by a populace for capital punishment and the placard-waiving "Abolish the death penalty!" counter-groups, were nonexistent on this early morning. There was something very medieval about the morning scene, troops encamped around a castle preparing to lay siege or storm the wall. Only in this case, the impenetrable fortress was the Utah State Prison, Maximum Security, Death Row facility surrounded by an electrified fence and topped off with concertina barbed wire.

Once inside Death Row we were escorted into the cellblock. It was unnerving to hear the heavy metal gates latch behind us. We'd crossed a threshold that very few outsiders ever had a chance to witness. The three of us were only feet away from some of Utah's most deadly criminals. Only when we were inside the relative safety of the interview room did we speak.

"Are you okay?"

"Yes," Lindsey answered. Josh shook his head affirmatively.

We double-checked all the equipment to make certain everything worked and then we waited. After a few minutes we heard the shuffling of chains and moments later the door opened. John Albert Taylor, escorted by two armed guards, entered the room. He was seated directly in front of the three of us and chained to the wall. What immediately struck me was that he was considerably heavier than his booking photographs, perhaps so by eighty to a hundred pounds. I introduced myself to Mr. Taylor and then introduced him to Josh and Lindsey. I asked him if we could take a photograph of him for our school newspaper and he agreed. Then he began to talk about his innocence in the murder of Charla King.

If I had any concerns or fears about Josh and Lindsey being intimidated by John Albert Taylor, they were quickly dismissed when both journalists caught Mr. Taylor in contradictory statements from his trial. Taylor protested his innocence throughout his trial, claiming that the only reason his fingerprints were on the telephone cord was because he had lifted up the phone to look for money that might have been tucked there by Charla's mother. Lindsey referred to his contradictory testimony at the trial and Josh followed up with a series of good solid questions pushing and challenging Taylor in ways, I'm certain, he had not expected. He wasn't prepared for the interview and Josh and Lindsey were. Instead of being interviewed by two high school journalists, Taylor was interviewed by two investigative reporters who happened to be on a high school newspaper staff from an alternative high school whose students had always been underestimated.

That year, *The Liberator* won the highest awards in high school journalism offered in the State of Utah and Josh and Lindsey took first place in investigative reporting. More important to all of us was the lesson Josh offered in dreaming and acting on the impossible. Josh and Lindsey refused to let anybody define who they were, and more significantly, who they would become.

Ghost Brother

It was three a.m. and the voice on the other end of the phone was small and distant. At first, I could not be certain.

"Hello?" (pause) "Hello?"

"Hello?" I felt anxious and nervous. It was deep into the night and the connection was scrambled. Slowly, I began to recognize the voice.

"Barry?" Echo in a deep canyon followed by the bullwhip crack of static. "Is that you?"

"Hello? Jeff? Is that you, Jeff?"

"Barry?"

"Jeff. (static, crackle, words dropped, fallen) . . . birthday."

Nothing.

Space and silence. Disconnected, I feared. Lost again and there was no way to contact him. He was calling from an internet café, somewhere.

"Hello? Hello? . . . Jeff? I thought we got disconnected."

"Are you okay, Barry? Are you in trouble?"

"Is this my only brother? My only brother, Jeff?"

"Yes. Yes."

"You are the only brother I have."

"Are you OKAY, Barry? Are you safe?"

"I left Costa Rica. I was robbed at gunpoint . . ."

"Where are you now?"

"Nicaragua. By a lake. They would have killed me."

Quickly. "Are you alright? Are you hurt?"

Muddled words, disoriented. Both of us, always with each other. Diagramed by dysfunction and demons.

"I need to tell you . . . you are my only brother. Do you know what I mean?"

I do and I want to tell him so. Still, it is not enough. Then silence. Absolute.

Again, my brother becomes a ghost. Swallowed by darkness. I can feel him in my chest.

It is a sad and simple story. A young man goes off to a foolish war and he returns home. But never really.

The Great Escape

It was an odd time for a phone call. Midday. Landline reserved for emergencies. The phone on my desk in the classroom was a hotline. The crispness of the ring cut the air. It held electricity and I could feel its teeth. My students looked at the desk, at the black phone, at me. I could only imagine. That feeling, that middle-of-the-night ring out of pitch dark, stomach-churning acid reflux where nothing could turn out right.

The second ring snapped me into movement. I turned my back slightly to the class. Answered. The voice, unfamiliar, nervous.

"Is this the caretaker for Mary Louise Metcalf?"

"Yes." Firm. Slightly annoyed.

"This is Danielle from Winthrop Manor."

"Yes."

"I don't know how to say this . . ."

"Say what?"

"It's about your mother. She's gone."

I'd thought about this moment many times over the last two years. My mother's brutal dance into the spiral darkness of Alzheimer's was finally over. I was relieved. Silenced. Measured.

(Pause) "It's a blessing." I tried to sound shaken and surprised. It wasn't true. I was relieved for her.

"Oh, no, I'm sorry. I don't think you understand. I'm not being clear."

"Excuse me?"

"About your mother."

(Confused) My creative writing class was interested. I turned my back completely, whispered.

"What are you talking about? I am in the middle of class here."

"I'm sorry. I can see how you would think . . ."

"What are you trying to say?"

"Your mother escaped."

Complete confusion. Processing . . . giddigeegick giddigee-gick, whirling hurly girly, pieces suspended, not fitting, tumblers sliding, suspiciously asked, out of context. I had no words.

"We don't know how she did it, but she did." As though that would explain it all. "One of the staff, Lupe, was out having a cigarette when she saw your mother . . ."

"Do what? What did she see her do?"

"Climb on the back of a motorcycle and ride off with a man."

"Tell me this is a fucking joke, Danielle, please tell me this is a joke."

San Quentin is easy. Alcatraz, if you can swim, possible. But the Winthrop Manor, north side, impossible. The south side, across the busy intersection of First South and Seventh East is where one enters into the system. It's billed as a "boutique community" where "you can live the same lifestyle that you have become accustomed to at home." It's true. Probably a better environment than many of the guests had previously experienced in their own homes.

The facility is well appointed, the staff, friendly and thoughtful. On the main floor, there's an impressive library with deeply comfortable wingback chairs and a phony gas fireplace that beckons. The dining room's large water feature bubbles calmly, surrounded by giant indoor trees, light spilling from a giant skylight, a piano with a pianist for dinner, chef-prepared meals, and dancing post dinner. My mother was a star. She danced and sang, flirted and teased, and the men loved her. And then, she began to slip. She got lost and couldn't find her way back. She would leave the television on full volume because the *off* and *on* buttons were too confusing. Then the stove top, burners left on high for two days until housekeeping alerted the administration. Then cigarettes. When the staff found her wandering on the rooftop wearing a Wonder Woman cape and very little else, they called me. It was fair. She'd become a risk to herself and others. It was time to move her to the north side.

In many ways, the north side of Winthrop Manor looks and feels much like the south side. It is airy and light with a main foyer that has large birdcages full of colorful exotic birds. The only difference, and it is palpable, is the feeling that nobody on the north side will leave the facility alive. When I would dine with my mother and her girlfriends at the south side, the conversation would invariably turn to so-and-so who had moved across the street to the "dark side." There would be a reverential silence, perhaps a moment for the passing of one companion into a world where they did not exist anymore.

People on the north side can't care for themselves. A twenty-four-hour staff graciously and delicately attend to their needs. Often, when I would go to visit my mother I would run into Carla, one of the staff who would bathe my mother. In her sweet Spanish accent she would say, "We all love your mother. She is one of our favorites." I could see this. My mother, among many things, was a warm and generous friend. In the throes of Alzheimer's, she had become a gifted actress, learning to cover her confusion and the disappearance of language by using short phrases designed to placate. "You're such a dear," and "Aren't you just the sweetest thing." What else does one really need to hear?

When my sister and I moved our mother across the street, we knew she wasn't happy. I am certain she understood what it meant and there was a deep and quiet anger. In a sense, at least in her world, we had betrayed her. We did our best to make her comfortable. We got help from a designer and appointed her room with all her favorite furniture and art. The space was comfortable and bright. It felt like her. Shortly before my sister returned to her family in New Mexico, my mother grabbed me forcefully by the arm until I turned to her. "I can get out. Don't think I can't." I never told my sister this. I thought about this now as I drove toward the Winthrop Senior Care Center.

When I arrived there were two patrol cars with lights whirring. A couple of officers were outside the facility talking with staff. I climbed out of my car, walked up, and introduced myself to the officer in charge. I asked what they knew about my mother's disappearance.

"We know that she got on the back of a Harley Davidson with a large man. They headed south."

"That's it?"

"So far." It wasn't a good answer.

I turned to the concierge who managed the front desk. "How did she get out? The front doors are always locked. Did you let her out?"

"No."

"Then how?"

"We think she snuck out the kitchen door when the cook was unloading freight."

"In other words, you have no fucking idea? Is that right?"

"Sir," interrupted the officer, "that attitude doesn't help us here."

"Really?" I could feel my filter disengaging.

"Does your mother have any friends who ride Harleys that might have dropped by to visit her? Does she know anybody in a . . ."

"In a damn motorcycle gang? Is that what you were going to say? Are you serious? My mother is seventy-nine years old, for Christ sake! Most of her male friends are dead! Jesus, you've got to be kidding."

"Sir, I'd like you to settle down so we can do our job and find out what really happened."

I think most people would say that I'm a fairly even-tempered person but this burlesque show short-circuited my wires. I began a colorful discourse that offered no way out for the officers but to probably have to subdue me, perhaps even taze me. I couldn't put on the brakes. I will never know exactly how things might have transpired if I kept on that trajectory because the beefy sound of a Harley Davidson cut through the afternoon air.

We watched as the Harley turned west from 700 East and roared into the driveway of Winthrop Manor. A brick of a man with full beard and riding leathers footed the kickstand and climbed off his hog. My mother, dressed in an all-yellow outfit, sat quietly on the Sundowner deep bucket seat wearing a matted black, old-school "brain bucket" helmet at least two sizes too large. She was smiling. Delicately, as though they were climbing out of a limousine for a high school prom, he offered my mother his hand. When she extended her hand he gracefully lifted her off his bike. She was smiling. It was a beautiful moment.

In a blur, the officers grabbed and began questioning him. I hugged my mother. When my mother saw what was happening, the confusion on the biker's face, she cried out, "Don't!" It silenced us all. "He took me to get the sticks with the red."

The officers stared at her. I translated for them. "French fries with ketchup," I said. "He took her to get French fries."

The officers pressed. Why had he picked my mother up? Did he have any idea how serious this was? Blah . . . blah . . . blah.

The biker wasn't rattled. I could sense he'd been down this road before. When he finally spoke he simply said, "She was hitchhiking up the street. I gave her a lift. She reminded me of my mother. I bought her an ice cream and some French fries."

I introduced myself to him and thanked him. "No worries. It was my pleasure." I stood alongside my mother until the officers let him go and then walked my mother into the safety of Winthrop Manor.

Full Circle

It has been twenty-six years since he has spoken with her, his ex-wife, and when he hears her voice over the phone it sounds like a confession. There is no salutation, as though, he imagines, she thinks he has thought of her every day. It seems to him there is still a touch of anger—no, jealousy—at the back of her throat, stuck. It makes him feel sad.

"I have some old photographs of you from when we first got . . ." There is a broken pause, one that feels like an olive branch. For him the war has been over for a very long time. "Anyway," she clears her throat, "I was cleaning out the office and there are some great pictures of your mother and father . . ."

"Yes," he says, cutting her off without meaning to. "I'd love them."

To him, it is a gift and he is touched by it. His children, when they were younger and still now but less frequently, had asked, "Did you ever have any hair? How come you don't have any pictures when you were young?"

"Yes, of course I had hair," and he would move the question along like so many other things about his past.

There is something about the phone call that seems completely final. He knows this, he senses it, but can't at this moment work it out clearly. It is so unexpected. Out of the blue.

"If you'd like, I could drop by your office and pick them up."

"I'll send a messenger."

"Okay," he replies. "But I'm happy to just swing by. It's not a problem."

"Our law firm uses messengers."

"I remember." An awkward beat, "I remember."

He hangs up the phone, closes the door to his university office, and begins to do the math, work the equation of this gift, hypothesizing in Xs + Ys.

Photographs – X = phone call (Nothing)

26 years – phone call = pictures (Blank)

He is not a mathematician, he teaches literature and playwriting. It makes no sense. Not now. After all these years. And he wonders how those photographs could have survived.

When he arrives home, his daughter is in the kitchen preparing a light dinner, pouring a glass of wine. His son lumbers into the frame. They both have questions. It is in their eyes.

"Dad, you remember my friend Andy?" his son asks.

"Of course," his father says, trying to find the face.

"He brought by an envelope for you today, from your ex-wife." Then, adding quickly to help turn the corner, as if it could explain all, "He works for a delivery service."

"Andy was surprised," his daughter said, "when he found out you'd been married to . . ."

"It was a long time ago," he replies, picking up the package and going into the den and, again, closing a door.

Delicately, he places the envelope on his desk, pausing for a moment before taking out a knife and carefully running its sharp blade along the seam. The photographs have a rubber band loosely wrapped around them. He sensed they had been arranged in a particular order for him, a code of sorts, the language of a gesture. Twenty pictures in all. Two for every year they had been married.

One photograph in particular—the only one out of order—of him, twenty-two years old, the same age as his daughter now, in a dark green, v-necked sweater, a white polo shirt with the collar turned up, his left arm leaning against the driver's side of their first brand new car—a yellow Volkswagen convertible—his right arm comfortably resting under his left, his hair gently blowing in the wind, a slight smile on his face at the house where they had first lived on Grace Street.

He remembered the picture always. Wondered, perhaps, if it too had disappeared in the seam, discarded . . . dissolved. The eyes had always puzzled him, though, still did—something in the gaze, the dark brown intensity of his eyes, laser-like, piercing through the camera lens. Those eyes were not of him.

Slowly, he gets up from the desk and walks to the mirror in the corner of his office, leans over and examines his face. There are scars and lines. He has lost his hair and his face is heavy, eyes weighted by the years, by the stories he carries. Holding the photograph against the mirror, he studiously takes inventory. He would have to admit, he'd grown out of everything and finally, at last, grown into those eyes.

Bone Deep

Last fall, a group of seventeen men, all strangers to each other, met for the first time to fly fish together at one of Utah's most pristine series of private trout ponds belonging to Falcon Ledge Lodge in Altamont, Utah. The men came from various parts of the state and were the guests of a program called Reel Recovery. The program brings men together for three days of fly-fishing and conversation about their lives, specifically, how they are dealing with their own cancer. If there is a catch, no pun intended, it's based on the simple idea that men, unlike women, need to learn how to talk about their own health issues. And men need to talk with each other. The program brings these men together where there are beautiful trout, teaches the art of fly-fishing, and invites them to talk.

I'd read about the program in Trout Unlimited and I was intrigued by the idea. Each participant would be paired together with a volunteer guide whose primary job would be to teach the basics of fly-fishing. For part of three days, the Reel Recovery participants would have their own private trout guide. I found this idea most appealing. For over forty years I have fished the great trout waters of Utah and thought that giving back in such a fashion was meaningful and important. Earlier in the year I had contacted Reel Recovery headquarters and offered my services as a guide. To my pleasant surprise I was given the dates, contact points, and directions to Falcon Ledge. On the given day, I was the first to arrive replete with extra waders, fishing vests, fly rods, reels, boxes of flies, and a variety of different-sized boots tucked into my kit.

I introduced myself at the front desk and waited for my instructions. It seemed logical that once the men arrived there would be some sort of general orientation and then perhaps the guides would be introduced to their partners. With that in the back of my mind, I was surprised when one of the facilitators welcomed me to the lodge and offered to show me to my room.

"I thought the guides either camped out or drove themselves to the retreat on a daily basis."

"That's right."

"Then I really don't need a room. I'm planning on camping out."

"But the Reel Recovery participants have a private room."

"I volunteered to guide," I replied, politely.

"Let's double check this," he said walking back to the check-in desk. After a few moments he looked up from his ledger. "We've got you down as a participant."

"I think there's a mistake."

"It says in the application that you have prostate cancer."

"I do. But actually, I signed up to guide."

"You filled out the wrong form. We've got you down as a participant."

"But . . . I don't think I need it. I'd rather . . ."

"Let me show you to your room and you can decide whether you want to stay or not. We'd love to have you join us."

Once I saw the view from the room it was all over. Beneath me, gently spread out in folds against the landscape, were several still ponds stocked with trout. A knuckle of a rise bubbled from a brown trout slurping a fly from an evening hatch.

"This is fabulous," I said. "I'd like to stay."

At the time, I had no idea that I was in need of such a retreat. This epiphany would be revealed to me in the coming three days. But, at that moment, the world seemed perfect. In the evening, we all met in a circle on the main floor of the lodge. In turn, we introduced ourselves to the group and answered a few questions about ourselves. The facilitators for the evening guided us along. The questions: simple enough. Name. Profession. Our favorite car growing up. Safe, manly stuff. Finally, just before we broke for dinner, a different direction, one I sensed would continue to be the focus of the remaining two days. What type of cancer do you have and how has it made you feel?

The responses were much more guarded and cautious because if we spoke truthfully and openly, we entered into the realm of self-revelation. This is not a place where men are comfortable being. It is too dangerous, too vulnerable. We have trained well to guard ourselves.

We were truly a mixed bag of men and there was little doubt we would have met under any other circumstance. Among our ranks were the president of a bank, a former cab driver, a retired railroad engineer, a lifer in the United States Army, a filmmaker, a professor of English, a plumber, a three-time world arm-wrestling champion, a brick mason, a Marine who did two active tours of duty in Vietnam, and a police officer. Two of the participants, Tuck, a retired railroad engineer, and Ed, his cousin and the world arm-wrestling champion, were two of the first men I met at the retreat. In the circle on the first evening, they sat to my left. Tuck, a handsome, rugged man, and Ed, who was at the time fighting three different cancers, were pretty vocal about not particularly being interested in this touchy, feely sort of public display of emotions. But the facilitators wouldn't allow that as a satisfactory answer. It became clear that silence, in carrying the weight of our own cancer, had not served any of us well.

Jim Cloud, one of the original founders of the Reel Recovery program, was pointed in his comments to the group. "I invite you during these three days to share your truth about cancer. The more you share this truth with each other, the more freedom you have."

After a few moments of uncomfortable silence, Cloud continued, "We share a legacy as men. We have gathered in circles for thousands of years to prepare for battles, to discuss strategy and purpose. Men have gathered after battles to discuss what worked, what didn't, and the men they lost. They have blessed each other, consoled each other, and rejoiced together in these circles."

The room became silent. At that moment, I realized this was more than I'd bargained for and this surprised me. I was in for something I needed deeply, and that was the theme: "courageous conversation of men with cancer." We studied each other to see who would pick up the gauntlet.

Finally, Ed broke the silence and began to talk about his cancer and how it had changed his life. He spoke of the pain he believed he had caused his family by having cancer. His voice was almost inaudible as he spoke of having to deal with something he couldn't conquer with his bare hands. "When I look at myself in the mirror and see all the scars on my body, I feel like Frankenstein. I don't know how my wife can touch me."

I watched his cousin Tuck, the most vociferous among us who had talked about not having any interest in the "circle jerk" of emotional intimacy, as Ed continued to speak. Tuck had his head down. His arms were resting on his knees and it was clear he was having a difficult time holding things together. In truth, he was not the only one in the group barely holding on. And then, Ed put us all over the top when he spoke of his two boys, Hunter and Fisher.

"I don't feel like I've been much of a father to my boys. They are having a difficult time with this and they're angry and I can't do anything about this. I feel worthless. I don't feel like a husband or a father, and sometimes," he stopped, wiping tears from his eyes, "I wonder if they wouldn't be better off without me."

Tuck began to cry. He reached over, and as gracefully and gently as I have ever seen one human being comfort another, he took his cousin's hand and squeezed it softly. From that moment on, we were all changed. Ed's utter self-revealing honesty, his laying out of his darkest and most intimate secrets in front of a group of strangers, was perhaps one of the bravest and most generous gifts I have ever witnessed or received. This simple act of charity disarmed us and granted us permission to tell our own stories. And we did. Each man in turn offered up what was most private and unspoken. I found myself talking about the most carefully guarded secrets in my dealings with cancer. Never could I have imagined.

The fly-fishing was brilliant. During the three-day retreat, all seventeen men caught fish. And in those sweet moments, the length of time between the cast and the rise of a plump trout to the fly, we were all free of our cancer.

I entered into the weekend with the belief that I would be a "buddy" to men who had cancer and had never fly-fished before. Had that been the case, I would have left the retreat with a feeling that I had given something of myself to men who were in need. Instead, it was I who was the recipient of their generosity and brotherhood. I realized that, indeed, I was in great need.

Five of the men I fished with have passed away since the beginning of this collection of short essays. Three or four others have had cancers return, including myself. Whenever I return to the river, I carry these men with me. When I catch a plump trout, I name it for one of my brothers and release it back into the wild where it disappears into the sacred and holy waters of my home water.

Unspoken

All rivers race to the heat of the heart, where water whispers a name
and a place, spreads itself flat, stops waving goodbye and returns to
reflect the green shore.
—*Roslyn Nelson*

For almost two decades I have marked my life by the April steelhead run on the Salmon River outside of Lower Stanley, Idaho, in the broad embrace of the Sawtooth Mountains' jagged granite teeth.

I have marked these years in equal measure of friendship, laughter, the escape from civilization, and the knowledge that I am, if only briefly, a guest in this ritual life dance of a dying species, the great ocean-going rainbow trout, the steelhead. Such illusionists of light and shadow, these anadromous steelhead travel over nine hundred miles to spawn in their original hatching grounds on the Salmon River. The biological need to reproduce. Such instinct for survival. The possibility of life. A beautiful thing, life.

For the past two days, temperatures outside the hand-hewn log cabin on Crooked Creek Ranch have not been above zero. This year, spring has refused to arrive and holds stubborn to the particulars of the land. A fire crackles in our cast-iron stove and the cabin breathes and sighs with its own winter songs. Stiff, dark coffee percolates in a battered pot, the aromatic smell of dark Arabian beans as seductive and mysterious as life itself.

I have arrived a few days before the others so Cole and I can fish together. We begin a slow and ritualistic chorus in preparation for the morning. The conversation is stripped of anything but the essentials. In all honesty, we have said it all before. Our morning chatter is liturgical and measured in ritual.

"It's going to be a cold one."

"Yes it is."

"I hope we can see them today."

"It'll be difficult."

"Yes it will."

And it will. These are true words. There is no room for anything else in this landscape of snow and ice, the gurgling of the Salmon River, and steelhead. This is a small part of the beauty. There is a reason I have arrived early this season to steelhead fish with Cole. I need to talk with him about my health, but in two days, I have said nothing.

To put these words into the universe makes me feel as though I will begin to disappear. My health issues are real enough. I am not a foolish man. There are medical facts and mathematical percentages and still, I can't help feel that there is medicine and magic in this water of equal weight.

In the rumble of water over rock, the Salmon River whispers to me of its own sacred medicine.

So, I say nothing.

The serpentine road downriver from lower Stanley is slick with a layer of snow-covered ice. We pay attention. Around the bend, a smashed sports car reminds us there are no second chances. Frozen rocks, loosened by the breathing of the canyon walls, have crashed onto the slender two-lane highway. A herd of elk dusted in snow huddles close to the road. A giant bull stands guard over the herd, measuring us for danger. And when our rig gets close enough to see into his deep mercurial eyes, he is done with us. We are not a threat and he turns away, toward the sweeping basin, toward the wolves. It has been a harsh, brutal winter this year in the Stanley Basin. The herd looks thin and weary and I say so.

Sixteen years ago, over a dozen wolves were released in central Idaho by the state's wildlife agency and protected through the federal Endangered Species Act. Immediately, lines were drawn between conservationists and local farmers and sheepherders. At the center of this maelstrom against the reintroduction of wolves into the landscape was a man by the name of Ron Gillett. Ron owns a very successful river-running company in Stanley, and Cole and I both know him. The rugged landscapes of the Sawtooth Mountains and the great Stanley Basin have provided him with a good living.

"Did you hear what happened with Ron and the Wolf Lady?"

"No," I replied, thankful for the distraction.

"You know how he hates the wolves?"

"Yes," I said, pouring us both a cup of coffee from a battered Stanley thermos.

"Well, he was driving into town when he sees the Wolf Lady taking photographs of wolves frolicking in the snow. Ron pulls his rig over, jumps out with his rifle and starts yelling at the Wolf Lady."

"You've got to be kidding!"

"So, the Wolf Lady turns her camera on Ron and starts shooting off pictures."

"And?"

"They got into some sort of scuffle. The Wolf Lady claimed Gillett tried to grab the camera from her. She ended up falling to the ground. They've been at it for some time."

"What happened?"

"Ron got thrown in the tank overnight. There'll be a trial in July or August."

"What do you think will happen?"

Cole blew on his coffee, took a sip, and chuckled.

"Stupid question," I admitted. Cole nodded his head. We both knew the outcome.

Four months later Ron Gillett walked out of a Custer County courtroom a free man. It was justice in northern Idaho. Nobody was surprised.

Winter months in this landscape can break even the hardiest of people. Stories are told and retold of townspeople who got cabin fever and just up and left, people who disappeared or committed suicide or drank themselves to death. It's rare, but it happens.

As an outsider these narratives beg questions: How and why does this happen? What is the pathology of this winter landscape? How do things fester in us? Is it one thing that becomes another and we finally snap?

There is a poison in Ron that does not fit how he has governed himself on the river. At the mention of healthy wolf packs he can hardly control himself. One of Gillett's frequent battle cries in preaching the anti-wolf gospel is, "We don't care if you nuke 'em or poison 'em, just as long as they're gone!" If possible, he would rid the West of all wolves. This frenzied madness plays well in this landscape of ranchers and sheepherders but it is hollow and vacuous. For Ron, it is consumptive and leaves little room for reflection and balance.

"It's like a cancer and it's eating Ron up. Them wolves."

There it was: the opening I needed to talk to Cole about the aggressive return of my own cancer. I'd promised my wife I would speak to the boys, to keep it all out front and on the table. I'd practiced what I would say and knew it would not be an easy conversation for either of us.

In the most profound and sacred of ways, Cole and I are brothers. We go deeper with each other than we do with our own kin.

Still, we tend to keep our emotional cards close to the table. I am good at this, but Cole is much better. I began slowly, trying to get the words right in my mind.

"Speaking of cancer . . ." I said, clearing my throat.

Cole interrupted me. "Pull over. A pair of steelhead."

I eased my rig off onto the shoulder of the road. Cole was out onto the pavement headhunting for steelhead before I could yank on the emergency brake.

"A male and a female."

"Where?"

"See the dead branch, directly across the river?"

"Just above the white pyramid rock?"

"Yes."

My eyes strained. I hadn't been back on the river long enough to shift to my steelhead eyes.

"Can you see them?" Cole asked.

"How far out from the pyramid rock?"

"On our side up about a rod length."

Again, I tried to focus. First I looked upstream, distracting myself by the canyon walls with the hope that I might then be able to see, as Cole often said, "the absence of what should be there." He didn't press me.

Seconds before I was about to confess I'd failed, the female fanned the redd. Moments later, a large male slid over and held to her side. We moved slowly, staying low and in the shadows, hardly breathing. Every so often, Cole stopped in his tracks and studied the river.

"Grab your rod and go cast to the male. I'll spot."

"That's not going to happen," I replied stubbornly.

"I've been up here a week, Metcalf. Go get your rod."

"Rock . . . paper . . . scissor," I suggested, pounding my fist into an open palm.

It's not that either one of us wouldn't die to be the first to cast to this large rogue male, but Cole's generosity is such that he will not fish until his friends have all cast.

Long ago, we'd resolved how to take care of such a problem. Rock, paper, or scissor. I threw down paper to Cole's rock.

I assembled my 8-weight rod. Cole selected a couple of flies and we talked about the best way to approach the male.

"We'll both cross the Death Wade. Drop below the male and work up river. I'll cross above and spot for you."

As we slid into the Salmon I began to tense up. Cole offered calm words.

"Take your time. No rush."

This area of the Salmon we refer to as the Death Wade and I am not fond of it. Because the canyon walls narrow significantly in this stretch, the current is often swift and treacherous. I pushed against the current trying not to lose my footing, which was already uncertain. The next fifteen feet of river demanded full attention. To slip here would be disastrous.

After working my way through the tongue, I paused and tried to settle down. Cole was already climbing up a scramble of rock on the other side.

For a moment, I closed my eyes. The sounds of the Salmon began to soothe and calm me. It is a transformation so absolute and complete that I knew the conversation I'd planned to have with Cole about my own health issues would likely not happen. I'd come home again. When I opened my eyes and looked to Cole, he quickly signaled me with his hands.

"Hold up. The male is moving."

Cole gestured to the water. The light from my vantage point was poor. In the general vicinity where Cole had pointed, the river suddenly erupted in a violent swirl of fins and tails. A small male had probably tried to slide alongside the spawning female.

"He'll be back," Cole yelled to me, "as long as she stays put or until he gets his ass kicked good. Let them settle down before casting."

I stood in the river, waiting. Sunlight began to appear and slowly cut a diagonal slash of light against the canyon wall. The river glimmered in deep-flecked grays and oranges, reflections from the tumble of river rock. The chorus of the Salmon became, at once, hypnotic and soothing.

"Ready to cast?"

"Yes."

"Can you see them?"

I nodded.

"Okay. Cast about three feet above them, almost against the bank and let the fly swing directly in front of them."

I pulled line off my 8-weight and let it float behind me until I'd reeled off what I thought I'd need for a proper cast. I made several false casts directly upriver until the line was measured and then I shot the line diagonally above the holding steelhead. It was a perfect cast, the weighted fly sliding directly in front of the male.

"Good to see you haven't forgotten how to cast," Cole yelled over the water, adding as he often does, "Again. Same place."

Again, I made the same cast. And again. And again. The pair held tight.

"Tie on something different."

"Something dark?"

"Your guess is as good as mine."

I withdrew a fly box from my vest, studied the collection of brightly colored steelhead patterns, and selected a Halloween fly. I tied it onto my tippet and crimped the hook. I submerged the tip of my fly rod into the river to break up the ice that had formed on the guides.

Again, I began false casting. When distance was stretched out, I shot the line exactly where I had placed several dozen unsuccessful casts. This time was different. The instant the fly passed close to the female, the male struck violently, the water exploding into silver crystals, and the run was on.

Instinctively, the steelhead torpedoed toward a cluster of giant angular granite boulders directly upriver trying to cut the fly line. If I couldn't properly work this magnificent steelhead soon, it would all be over in seconds. Line screamed through the reel. I tightened the drag.

"Can you turn him?" Cole yelled.

"I don't know!"

The brutal raw strength of this steelhead was stunning. The steelhead exploded through the surface of the water into a cartwheel and slowed for just a second.

"If he gets wrapped around those rocks, he'll bust you off."

I knew that. I was getting dangerously close to the backing on my reel. I leaned hard on my fly rod and tightened the drag to a dangerous point; but the steelhead wasn't tiring. My arms were starting to feel the burn. For a split-second, the steelhead seemed unable to make any headway and, under the impression I had some control over this moment, I relaxed. The steelhead reversed directions and bee-lined directly toward me. Madly, I stripped line as rapidly as I could. In an instant, the steelhead jetted by me and made an abrupt cut to the tongue of the river where the current could be worked against me.

"Jesus! Did you see the size of him?"

"You've got to chase him downriver or you'll lose him. See if you can work him to the bank. I'll head downriver and see you in Challis," he cackled before making his way to the bank, grabbing his large steelhead net and hustling downriver. Cole hollered something from the bank. Although I couldn't hear him, I have some sense of his advice. "Keep your rod tip up!"

In truth, this steelhead was getting the better of me. I took off downriver trying to keep my feet spread apart and balanced. Stumbling at this point in my footing would be disastrous.

Quickly enough I was in the seam of fast water, exactly where I didn't want to be. I was moving into treacherous water and I'd lost sight of Cole. In a way, I was relieved because he would be chiding me about "going for a swim if I didn't turn the steelhead soon.

A sudden shift in footing and I stumbled into the Salmon. I struggled to keep upright. Bent almost to the knee, water topped the bib line of my waders and a slosh of freezing water streamed into my boots. It could have been worse. I could have gone under.

Somehow in the chaos, I managed to keep the rod tip upright and the steelhead on. Slowly, I regained my composure and settled down to matters at hand. Cole was a speck downriver, descending a steep shale slope to where he believed I'd be able to land the steelhead. I had some good luck, the steelhead swung in a huge arch from the deep water and moved into a stretch of current I thought I could handle.

My fly line grew taut and hummed its own particular music as the steelhead cut downriver toward the proper side of the bank. Then, surprisingly and instinctively, he began a slow, determined course upriver toward the female's redd. This shift gave me valuable time to gain slack line back onto my reel.

When the steelhead was parallel to me, I got my first good close look at him. He was magnificent with thick shoulders, a deep steel blue cast along his back and head, with a wide, rich crimson, almost burgundy stripe along his side. I could clearly see the fly, sunk deep into his jaw.

There was a slight slack in the line and I was cautious not to reel it taut until I could move closer to the bank and gain better footing. A slight twist in my footing rumbled rocks and the male shuddered. I braced for what I expected to be a run. Instead, the steelhead pulled parallel to the female and held.

He was spent. In what must have felt like his final moments in the Salmon River, this steelhead refused a last run and, in turn, followed a deep biological instinct to complete a life cycle.

Slowly, I was able to get to the bank, firm up my footing, and land the steelhead. He was a massive steelhead, talon scarred across his back, a chunk chomped from his tail, firm and taut and spent. I took him back to the water, held his tail, held my thumb on his lower jaw, and moved him slowly, back and forth in the current, talking to him and offering thanks before releasing him into the safety of the Salmon River.

I sat on the bank and looked downriver as Cole waved his approval. I closed my eyes and savored this moment with deep appreciation and respect. In this instant, my world was as close to being perfect as I could hope for.

I thought of my early morning awkwardness in trying to talk to Cole about my health. In truth, what did I really need to tell my best friend? Would I say that my surgery, radiation, and hormonal treatment had not been successful? Did I need to tell Cole that, in all probability, we would not get as much time to fish together as either of us would like? I suspect, in his own way, Cole already knew these things.

When he joined me at the bank of the Salmon River I told him the only truth I really knew. "That, my friend, was a noble steelhead."

"Yes it was," he replied. He dug inside his steelhead jacket, pulled out a pack of Marlboro lights, and offered me one. After a few moments of silence, he said, "It's good to see you again." All I could say in reply was, "And the same back to you." It was all that was necessary.

Early Morning Blues

It is 3:40 a.m., and I have padded down to the study. The house is quiet, and the only noise is an old fan circulating dead air in the room.

For the last five weeks I have been involved in a protocol for treating advanced prostate cancer. The protocol is called Provenge (sipuleucel-T) and it is designed to train your body's immune cells to seek out and attack prostate cancer cells.

One might say that Provenge is a designer drug. I go to the local Red Cross plasma center to receive a leukapheresis procedure. Needles are inserted into both my arms in solid veins. One needle pumps blood into a machine where it is separated into different components. The separation of immune cells, platelets, and red blood cells are collected in a plastic bag and the remainder of the blood returns through the other needle back into my body. The process can take up to four hours and during the process one is expected to remain motionless to the best of their ability.

It is not easy to do.

The bag of extracted cells is carefully packed into an overnight box and mailed off from the Red Cross plasma center to one of three locations in the country where a cocktail will be developed using one's own cells. My immune cells will be activated with recombinant antigen cells that will attack the prostate cancer cells.

"By stimulating the natural ability of immune cells already in your blood, Provenge may help you live longer." I hold to this last line.

Three days after the immune therapy cocktail has been designed and returned to the cooperating hospital, you are infused with this mixture. There can be serious reactions to the infusion including headaches, back pain, chills, fatigue, and nausea. I have had all of these reactions. I would add another and that would be sleeplessness.

I am headed into the ninth year of dealing with prostate cancer and I have, based on early predictions, cheated death for many years. I'd like to continue to do so.

I like it here on earth.

We have a daughter who is ready to deliver her first child and a son who is beginning to stretch out into the world seeking his place.

I have undergone more treatments, protocols, and clinical trials than I can remember and I don't know my body anymore.

This morning, only hours ago, I took off all my clothes and stood naked in front of a full-length dressing mirror. There is nothing here I recognize. I have absolutely no body hair. My muscle tone had disappeared and I retain water. I've developed breasts that in the seventh grade would have been the envy of any young girl.

Perhaps most difficult to look at is my penis. It doesn't belong to me. I don't know what happened. It could have been something during my radical prostatectomy, but it is not the same penis I began with. Fact. I was circumcised before the operation and afterward—let me say this—I wasn't.

Emotional things begin to stack up, one thing upon another, and I find myself crying. It is a deep and wounded sound and it is the first time this has happened to me during this entire journey. I am making sounds that I don't recognize. I am afraid that I might awaken my wife so I quickly try to put my sweats back on, accidently place both feet into one pant leg, and start to fall over.

On the way down, I grab onto a small coffee table laden with books hoping it might brace my fall. It doesn't and I am left in a pile of books: *Unseen America, Weegee's World, Vietnam: A Complete Chronicle of the War*, and *Fish Flies: The Encyclopedia of the Fly Tier's Art*.

Still, I think, I am here. I will sit back up, dress myself, try to keep a balance, and hope on the far side of hope that I will be able to stay above the water.

Queen of Hearts

The night before I underwent surgery for the removal of my prostate gland, I had a strange dream. I thought about telling my wife
on the early morning drive to St. Mark's Hospital but I didn't.
What was there to gain by doing so and how could this possibly
serve her in any conceivable way? Up to this point in the discovery
of a rising PSA number, the need to have a biopsy performed, and
the subsequent discovery of cancer, I had remained steadfastly and
foolishly quiet. Although I thought it was the noble and manly
thing to do, it was, in all regards, a selfish decision.

In the dream I was with my wife at the French Laundry in
Napa Valley. Thomas Keller's restaurant. I'd just finished a luscious
cauliflower panna cotta with Beluga caviar and my wife, and I'm
pretty certain of this, was reaching for her Duck Fois Gras au
Torchon with pickled cherries when the next course and wine
pairing was delivered to our table. Such service! Such flavors!

We were having this great conversation and while she was
telling me this hilarious story about a client, this hand reached
over my shoulder and took a Parmigianino Crisp filled with Goat
Cheese Mousse. The first one didn't bother me, but when this
happened a second time, I grabbed the hand. Enough, already . . .
it was bad form. This was not right. These were EXPENSIVE hors
d'oeuvres, even for a dream.

"What do you think you're doing?" I asked angrily.

"I'm sorry, I've always wanted to eat at Keller's restaurant. I love his work—the sauces, his reductions, and presentation! It's legendary!"

I did not like his looks. There was something disturbingly familiar about him, and it isn't my habit to be rude but I pushed a bit.

"You had trouble getting reservations, too, eh? It's a bit early for a Halloween costume party, isn't it?"

His response was short and curt, "This isn't a costume."

"You're DEATH?" I asked.

"Umm . . . hmmm."

"Seriously?"

"Yes."

I glanced around the room and noticed that during our exchange, the room had shifted slightly.

"Where did my wife go? And the woman who was sitting at the table next to us? And the older gentleman eating by himself? And the wine steward?"

"They went back," he replied focusing directly on me. He seemed bulky and crooked as I studied him.

"Without the main course? Are they crazy?" I thought these were witty lines but DEATH did not smile. It annoyed me some. "But you're still here."

"I'm DEATH. I'm always here. Close by."

I couldn't help but laugh. DEATH was so serious and it all seemed a bit ridiculous. "That's funny. *'I'm DEATH.'* It's good material, really."

"You don't seem afraid."

"Should I be? We're between courses. My wife has gone to powder her nose. The wine is fabulous. She'll be back."

DEATH blinked and looked about.

"Look, I'm going to order another bottle of wine. Please, sit down and join me for a glass."

DEATH was caught off guard. "I've never been invited to join anybody for a glass of wine before."

I kept pushing. "Really? A guy like you? Get out of here . . ."

DEATH sat down at the table, lifted a napkin up, and tucked it into his collar just like my grandfather Walter used to do at every Sunday dinner. The gesture was uncomfortably familiar.

"People don't seem to like me."

"Seriously? People don't seem to like you?" I found myself getting annoyed at DEATH. "You walk around touching people on the shoulder and they drop dead. Of course they don't like you! And then there is the OUTFIT. Lose the look! Get rid of the hood and the scythe. You've got to change with the times."

Finally, as if figuring out the decoder ring, I asked, "Did you come for me?"

DEATH stood to full height and replied, "It's not entirely my decision."

"I'm interested in knowing. I'm curious. Tell me," I replied.

DEATH leaned toward me and began to sing a song, and then my wife awakened me.

"It's time for us to go, honey. How did you sleep?"

At first examination of the dream it appeared as if nothing of importance or consequence could be revealed in the telling. So, I didn't. Logically, from my end, it all deconstructed on the opening line. Every line begs challenge. I've never been to the French Laundry. I've read of Keller's culinary skills and I admire his exactness of repetition, but I've never experienced a cauliflower panna cotta with Beluga caviar or ever imagined Duck Fois Gras au Torchon with pickled cherries. The dream is weak, the plot nonexistent, and the dialogue, particularly mine, works toward the cheap punch line. It should have been the type of dream that could be immediately dismissed in the morning. Yet, the dream remained in body memory. It was a discomforting dream to silently carry into surgery and even more distressing to reappear post-surgery. When I began to function properly again, I wrote the dream down in a journal that I keep on cancer and left it alone.

Death appeared in a second dream when a patient I'd come to know during post-surgery radiation died. Our radiation schedules were similar so we developed a casual relationship as we changed clothes into hospital gowns before radiation treatments. Between the fifth and sixth week of our eight-week treatment, something changed in him. When I asked him how he was doing, he mentioned he was no longer interested in the fight. He'd had a good life and felt the time was right to stop going on and he wanted to make that decision on his own. I encouraged him to stay the course because we only had a couple more weeks left of radiation and matters were bound to improve.

The dream unfolded in a completely different fashion. There were fewer disturbances in the narrative this time. The following excerpt came directly from my cancer journals.

March 6

I saw Bill Carney for the first time in a couple of weeks. I didn't recognize him. The Marlboro Man had become a hollow shell. The chemo/radiation combination had been brutal. I almost walked by him. He was the color of death.

"Just walk on by, Professor. Don't say nothing."

"Beg your pardon?"

"It's me. Bill."

"Bill?" I felt awkward for not recognizing him. "How are you doing?"

"Not so good. I'm going to quit all of this."

"You can't."

"Who's to say?" He took a labored breath. "It should be me."

"Bill, we're almost done. A couple of more weeks . . ."

"I ain't the same. I'm done, Professor."

March 13

I asked about Bill Carney. I brought him a book of Robert Service poems. I thought he'd get a kick out of them. Maybe he'd relate to Service's poem, "The Men Who Don't Fit In." I asked one of the male nurses about him.

"I'm looking for Mr. Carney. Has he been in for treatment today?"

"He died."

"Bill Carney? The man was here last week."

"I know who you're talking about. Yesterday. He just quit. Sometimes people just give up."

I completely and utterly lost it. "Damn it . . . you're talking about a man here. An acquaintance of mine. Don't you ever talk about anybody just quitting! What the hell do you really know about Bill Carney or any of us? HUH?"

I was certain that I scared him. "Geez. Mister, I'm sorry. . . . I didn't mean anything."

I stormed out of the hospital. After recounting the experience of the afternoon to my wife, my dreams that night were extremely vivid.

I was sitting at a blackjack table in Vegas playing twenty-one. The dealer had been giving me sweet cards. I was winning. The booze was flowing. Scotch. Good stuff. I'd picked a hot table. Electric. Sometimes that happens when you're playing. When it does you stay at the table and work. I was sizzling. People were gathered around me. The house brought in a cooler. A new dealer. Somebody to cool down the table. To take the heat off the cards.

"Good evening, sir."

"Is it? It's hard to tell in here without any clocks."

"Touché. You've had the cards tonight."

"I'd like to keep it that way. It's gotten cold since you sat down. I think I'll cash in."

"That's a poor choice of words around me."

"How so?"

"You don't recognize me, do you?"

"We've never met. I'm good with faces."

"I followed your advice. People don't seem to like me and you said . . ."

"You walk around touching people and they drop dead. You're DEATH."

"You gave me good advice. I appreciated it. Look, I've had my teeth capped and I'm feeling good about myself lately."

"I'm glad I could help, but you still smell."

"There's no need to be rude. I was trying to thank you."

"It's what you are, what you do. You can't change it." Then, for the second time, I asked, "Are you here for me?"

"It's not that easy. I tried to tell you that before."

"You're a dream. It's a simple question."

"I'm DEATH. You're not afraid."

"No."

"People lie."

"We die in many ways."

"It's just a matter of time."

"Do you enjoy screwing with me?"

"Such anger, Professor."

DEATH was annoying me. I grabbed a full deck of cards and pushed them toward DEATH. "Cut the cards. Winner takes all."

"Your odds aren't good."

"I've heard that before."

DEATH toyed with the cards.

"Sooner or later you'll lose."

"Cut the cards!"

"If not now . . ." DEATH lifted the cut and studied the card, turned it toward me and laughed.

"A queen. The Queen of Hearts. Your turn."

I cut the deck and selected a card, pushed it toward Death, and walked away.

DEATH lost control.

"Come back. You didn't look at your card! Come back and flip the card over! This is not how you play this game! Come back right now! You can't make up your own rules!"

This dream unnerved me unlike the first. DEATH had slid into the second dream well disguised and I had carelessly dropped my guard. This had never happened to me in the dream world. Written down in my journal some months earlier where I could actually decipher and analyze the first sequence of DEATH it was laughable, but in this dream a transformation had occurred and DEATH was close by.

A good friend of mine, the late Utah poet laureate Ken Brewer, had been in correspondence with me via email when he was diagnosed with terminal pancreatic cancer at the same time I'd been diagnosed with advanced prostate cancer. Following the dream, I called him to see how he was doing. On this particular afternoon I was able to talk with him. His voice sounded strong and he told me his work was going extremely well. The irony of it all.

When I told him about my dream and asked him how he'd been dealing with his own mortality, he replied that it was important to use cancer and death as a lesson. And this is my own impression, but what I think he offered me was the gift of placement. Where could I place death without it becoming the theme in my life?

"Put it to work, Jeff. Put death to work." Ken followed our conversation by emailing me a draft of his poem "The Visit," which begins in the following manner:

> Death sits on the side of my bed
> skirt hiked to the hair line, says
> Hi handsome. Dance with me?
> No thanks, I say, not yet.

I'm just a man with pancreatic cancer, not a corpse.
Besides, I'm married.
Death stands and straightens his skirt.
I'll be back, marriage or not.

I took Ken's advice and stuck DEATH into a one-man play, *A Slight Discomfort*, that I'd been commissioned to write for the Salt Lake Acting Company. That way, I could keep my eye on the dream. The play is about my journey through cancer and it is extremely difficult for me to watch. I see myself onstage struggling with my own mortality while battling himself as much as he does the cancer. I see a man who has attempted to shield his family from the inevitable, and in doing so has done just the opposite. But it is just a play and it ends on a positive and hopeful note. But I know the truth and I still conceal it from my family and myself. The play no longer belongs to me.

DEATH as a character works. It always draws an uncomfortable laugh from the audience in its first appearance, but by the second appearance, toward the end of the play, the audience is at full attention. They are present and inside the play, translating this moment in the theatre into a personal and familiar narrative of their own experience. My character, the onstage Jeff, has become somebody close to them. The play is no longer about prostate cancer. It is about the human condition, about wanting to be treated with dignity and respect. *We are not alone! We are not alone!* Therein, I believe, lies the success of the play. Everybody leaves the theater, the package is tidied up, and we go home wanting to love what is close to us.

No matter in what city we perform the play, I stay after the curtain drops and the crowd leaves. I wait until the lights in the house are turned off just to make certain there are no shadows about. I turned my back on DEATH without looking at my card and I cannot be so reckless again. *It's just a matter of time.*

Split Second

Winter came late this year and when spring arrived early, the runoff in the Wasatch Mountains came hard and fast. The Provo River, the Weber River, and the Logan River were at their highest levels in over three decades. Such a spring makes fly-fishing difficult. The configuration of these rivers no longer feels familiar to me. Instead, these waterways have been forced through the violence of the runoff to accommodate this turbulent flow, and the result is a new geography. Farmland has been flooded, huge cottonwood trees have fallen into the rivers, and most of the water is a chocolate soup that roils over rock and cliff in angry symphony.

These waters are my sanctuary and I fish them more than most. In a good year I will fish over 120 days. In truth, these rivers have saved my life on more than a few occasions.

This year, because of my disheartening medical news, I've needed the river more than ever. I've found myself becoming anxious and snappy around my family. I wake up in the middle of the night unable to go back to sleep. So as not to disturb my wife, I pad into the study and read or find myself in the kitchen making stock and homemade soups. The kitchen is another way I keep my demons at arm's length. For the sake of my family and myself, it was essential that I chase water.

Patrick Tovatt is a hopeless fishing slut like myself. It took a life-affirming conversion from alcohol and drugs to fly-fishing to clear his pipes. A former soap opera star, he spent twenty-five years with major television studios, and when he needed it most, he found religion in fly-fishing. He surrendered himself to this higher order and it saved his life.

The first time we ever fished together was almost three decades ago and he was still drinking hard. When Tovatt stopped drinking and smoking, he did it cold turkey. He took some of his "soap" money and purchased a beautiful place on the Beaverkill River in New York where he tied flies and fished himself back to life. He's a tall, rugged man, athletic, muscular, and even at seventy-two, he's not somebody you'd want to pick a fight with. A gritty guitar player with a twisted sense of humor, Tovatt recently cut a satirical album, *Plain & Nothing Fancy*, lambasting right-wing politicians. His music is "old school" throwback to yesteryear's political comedians and he makes no apology for the unbridled lyrics in his music. He protests for causes he believes in, kicks the people who kick dogs, and is one of the most well-read people I've ever known. What I most appreciate about Tovatt is that he's a man who isn't afraid to stay in the room. I consider him one of my brothers.

So on the morning when I most needed to hear his voice, he called. My cell phone was, as is often the case, somewhere. I could hear it ringing but couldn't locate it. I punched in the message retrieve and heard his voice. "Hey, professor, just calling to check in and see how you're doing. You're probably in church (the river) preaching to the choir (trout). Give me a call when you get a chance."

I called Tovatt immediately and confessed that I was in a deep funk and needed to find some fishable water. Nothing more was necessary, and after listening to me he said, "I'll pack up and head out tomorrow. I'll see you in a couple of days."

When Tovatt's ex-wife packed her things and moved from New York to the west coast, taking their son with her, Tovatt folded up camp, packed his fly rods, and sold his Beaverkill home to fashion designer Tommy Hilfiger. He relocated to Grant's Pass, Oregon, where he could be next to their son. He and his wife had met each other in an AA meeting and union was not a good idea. Again, water calmed. His new home sat above the Rogue River where he could follow the migration of steelhead.

It takes Tovatt two days to drive from the Rogue to my home in Salt Lake City. When he arrived, we ate together with my family around our kitchen island. It's a comfortable and embracing space that invites stories and laughter. That night, there were plenty of both.

Early the following morning we departed on a path that took us to one of Tovatt's guitar buddies whose family owned a cabin outside of Lava Hot Springs. From the deck of the cabin we took in the sweet smell of sage and studied the broad sweep of land that unfolded before us like a quilt. Across the valley, an old John Deere sickle mower made slow loops around fertile hay fields in a hypnotic drone. And to our left, slipping down an Aspen-lined ravine, a beautiful doe grazed on lusciously thick grass. Occasionally, she would freeze, raise her head slowly, cock her ears, and listen for the unusual before returning to her feed. This landscape was deep balm for our souls.

We did the things one does in a small town. We stopped by the local fly shop, ate at the local cafe, picked up some flies, talked about the Portneuf, discussed the high river flows that western states had been victim to, inquired about good access spots to the river, and because of the ritual, were offered a couple of the owner's favorite places to fish. This came at the last minute along with a country map sketched on a piece of scrap paper.

Our first glimpse of the Portneuf confirmed what we'd already suspected: this small serpentine tributary of the Snake River was flooding over its banks. Access to stretches that looked decent were roaring tongues of mud and fanned out into coffee-colored flats. At several access points, the water was impossible to enter due, in part, to heavy brush and the expanded runoff. Perhaps, had we fished these stretches before, we might know how to enter the water, holding tight to the bank knowing there might be solid ground under foot. Stepping into unknown water on such a runoff would be disastrous. Instead, we continued upriver to a braided spot of the Portneuf, until we found some water we could work.

It was skinny water, surprisingly clear and shallow, and the casting was dreamy. I was upriver from Tovatt and would look back periodically to see him casting to small rises. In the early evening light, golden against the vibrant slopes of green pastureland, the world suddenly righted itself as it always does on the river. Occasionally I would hear a howl when Tovatt missed a fish or, still better, a cackle when he hooked one. Soon I disappeared into my own rhythm, my Winston 3-weight in hand and a box of dry flies in my shirt pocket. I felt at peace.

Following a hearty dinner we sat on the cabin deck and marveled at the quiet. A young buck with fur-covered antlers nibbled sweet leaves, oblivious to us both. I crept off the deck and worked downwind of the buck, wondering how close I could get before being detected and before the buck bounced off and disappeared. Tovatt offered hand signals and by taking short steps, staying hunched over and tight to the graveled road and protected by a slight cutback, I closed the distance. Remarkably, the buck would see me frozen in place and hold me in its gaze without fear or concern. My legs began to spasm and burn from the posture I held. And finally, when the buck deemed I was of no significance, it would bend its head downward and begin to eat again. I would rise up, check Tovatt's directions, and try to close the gap.

At a point no more than fifteen feet away, I stopped and stood upright. The buck rose up again, and again held me in its gaze. His tail twittered, his ears alert, and I could see his face full on, deep dark eyes directly locking onto mine. He chewed slowly, stopping occasionally to mark me. I opened myself up and whispered to him softly, thanking him for this moment. I was both transformed and transfixed by this calm. Something unlocked inside me and I felt the presence of everything holy and sacred in the natural world flood through me and into a larger universe.

I thought of my family: my daughter, pregnant with our first grandchild; my wife, Alana, who has been at my side for almost thirty years; and of my gentle son, John, who was getting ready to stretch out into the world in the artist's way. I thought of my brother, Barry, who had disappeared many years ago into the deep mystery of Nicaragua; and of my sister, Sue, who has helped me in the most difficult moments of my life. I thought of my friend Tovatt standing watch, who knew instinctively when to appear in my life; and the Captain, and Selvage, and Wells, and Kranes, and Max—great men all who have helped shape me in the most profound of ways.

In this moment I was awakened again to the verity that my life has been a gift and that all of it, behind me and in front of me, was and is on borrowed time. I exhaled deeply, expelling dangerous toxins, and inhaled the most heavenly of smells of sage, sweet berries, mowed hay across the valley, and the rich gumbo of soil and humus. Knots unraveled in my shoulders, layer upon unhealthy layer, and I felt an emotional portal unlock. I was beginning to tear up when the buck suddenly startled, bouncing off toward the road.

The Portneuf River was a bust so we decided to fish Chesterfield Reservoir, a sixteen-hundred-acre body of water in southeastern Idaho between Pocatello and Lava Hot Springs. Over the years, Chesterfield had quietly gained a reputation among fly fishermen for its large rainbow population. Chesterfield, like the Portneuf River the day before, was unfishable. The wind howled across the reservoir and whitecaps curled and marched across the water. It would be suicide to enter the water. Long in the face, we returned to the cabin, collected our kits, and took off for an afternoon at Lava Hot Springs.

That evening, after a relaxed day of floating in the hot springs, a massage that left us both drunkenly slothful, and a good dinner, we shifted gears and decided it was time to chase some good fishing elsewhere. I called the Captain who lived only twenty minutes from Silver Creek to see how the creek was fishing. The report for the Big Wood River echoed the common refrain of western waters. Unfishable. Silver Creek, however, was fishing very well, so the following day we packed our gear and headed for Silver Creek.

Two days on Silver Creek in float tubes catching big angry browns on tiny, tiny flies cannot be adequately described. To say that it was unbelievable and the fish we caught were hot and game is hardly a measure at all. It's a very small part of the equation. What offers permanence to the memory is all the events and landscapes one travels before and after the adventure. For a significant number of western waters, the hope of spring fly-fishing this year had been brutally dashed by the forces of nature. So, to find ourselves in the great company of men we admired and respected, on a spring creek of great reputation, in weather that transfigured into chameleon land and light was more than we could have hoped. And that in the course of a single day we would be exposed to whorls of light powdery snow, dazzling rainbows of such color and clarity it looked as though they dipped into Silver Creek itself, and rumbling, brooding clouds that shouldered atavistic myth, was, in itself, an offering of great benevolence.

Our drive back to Salt Lake was equal parts of animated conversation related to the previous two days of fishing and stretches of silence where each of us dissolved into our own private thoughts. Tovatt, I suspected, was thinking about his own son, a wonderful young man who was functionally autistic and trying to work things out in a complicated world, and I, in turn, was thinking about a procedure that, if successful, might garner me two months to two years of quality life.

We'd just pulled out of Shoshone headed south on a two-lane highway when two large deer bounded across the road directly in front of us. So close and fast, fully stretched in blinding speed, that I had a fraction of a second to make a wheel correction to avoid hitting them. It was instinctual, without thought, and I split the space between deer avoiding what we later realized would have been a horrendous accident. The highway beveled down a steep incline and we would most certainly have plummeted, end over end in my Subaru Forester, or worse still, run head on into oncoming traffic, a bloody mix of flesh and metal.

When my head cleared and I settled down, I thought of all of it, of the capriciousness of life, of how one thing might lead to the next, or not, of how all things hang precariously on reflex and circumstance. I thought of how a second sooner or later might have altered our lives and the promise of life forever. It framed for me a sense of happenstance and chance. There are no guarantees for any of this and what we believe we have in front of us cannot be played out with any certainty. Life was reduced to the simplest equation and I could live with this. Whatever time I would be granted, I would enjoy as I always had, in the company of my family and friends, all of whom have offered me love and light and laughter in the embrace of life.

Lay Me Down

Death has been on my mind lately. There have been my own medical reasons, of course, but that is not all of it. It is both larger and smaller than the scope of the inevitable. I have unexpectedly lost friends this year—great people who are supposed to be here but aren't—and this is bitter. It is difficult to accept.

I suspect it has a great deal to do with the lack of the steelhead season as well. If I am completely truthful about it, I am more worried about the Earth than I am about myself. When you are of a place and you carry it in your bones for a lifetime, you can see and feel even the subtlest changes after thirty years.

I have been married to the landscape of Stanley, Idaho, and the Salmon River for that long. And every year as the months grow closer to April steelhead season, the chatter between the Captain and me picks up. We will talk with each other early in the mornings because neither of us sleeps well until we are on the water in the company of each other and the company of our other steelhead brothers. We have performed this spring ritual for more years than I can easily remember. The talk centers on the essentials: temperature, sudden fluctuation of river conditions, clarity of the water, forecasts for the coming week, snow conditions, human traffic on the water, and, most important in the equation, the steelhead count from the Sawtooth Fish Hatchery.

The Captain lives for steelhead fishing and during the year works hundreds of overtime hours so he can take the month of

April off to do what he most loves to do, fly-fish for steelhead. We have generous friends who offer up their beautiful ranch on Crooked Creek that will house us for a good part of the month. If we are fortunate, they will join us as we fly-fish, eat well, and drink healthily together during much of that time. It is a lifeline away from the outside world and it takes off the pressure, at least momentarily, from the toxins. We meet together to fish because it takes us deeper.

I am fortunate because I can also make accommodations to fish for two weeks in April and I am even greater in fortune because my wife has always understood the importance of this ritual. My wife teases me about my excitement and I often feel like a young schoolboy completely packed and ready for the first summer camping trip.

Early weather reports have the Captain concerned. The Stanley Basin and particularly the upper reach of river we fish has been seeing unusually warm weather. The climate in the past ten years has changed noticeably and it's foolish to deny the science of global warming. The body of evidence is too indisputable. The Salmon River has become more unpredictable each year and that presents its own set of dangers.

If the temperature rises too quickly and doesn't freeze at night, the canyon spills tons of mud and silt into the Salmon River, making it impossible to see beneath the surface of the water. The river becomes, at first, tea colored and then coffee brown. Because our style of fly-fishing requires that we must be able to see the steelhead, to spot them, a runoff of this sort will be the end of the season. Even under the most ideal conditions, in the best years, the weather is always a gamble. Steelhead are difficult to spot. They are so beautifully camouflaged in their silver bodies against the glint of the river's underbelly, that it takes a trained eye to unlock the water. The Captain has such eyes and has taught us all to read the water.

After the Captain gets settled into the cabin, cuts a path through the snow and ice, stacks firewood for the month, and makes it comfortable for us, he heads off to the river to stalk steelhead. In the evening he reports on his findings and I hang onto the conversation like coded words in some sacred language of steelhead. To an outsider it would sound like pure gibberish, but to me, I can see exactly the spot and hold of water in this layered text.

"Nothing at the Fish Factory yet. Death Wade is still too shallow and the water is thin at the dump." Not only does this inform me of the water level, identifies an exact location, offers me an idea of the fish count, and gives me clinical observations of the river, but it paints a complete narrative of what I can expect.

But this year there is gravitas in his voice that I have not heard before. It is tangible in the tone and I am hoping that I have misunderstood what I have come to sense is the inevitable. Finally, less than a week before I am to depart for the Salmon River, in a late-night phone call, I know I am on the far side of hope.

In such weather, the Salmon River is dangerous and deadly. The difference between being here, in the moment, or not can be a simple misstep in the rush and pulse of water, an ill-timed cut of the paddle in a raft, a giant cottonwood tree splayed up against a bridge abutment, bare branches reaching out, beckoning like sirens just around the bend.

"The water is running high and fast and you know how dangerous that can be."

I certainly did and I instantly had a flashback to a moment many summers ago when I was running a writing workshop for at-risk high school students in Stanley, Idaho, and almost drowned on the Salmon River. I still get chilled thinking about it. Mid-week of the conference we would take our students on a half-day river trip beginning at Mormon Bend and taking out below Sun Beam Dam. For several years, Ron Gillett, owner of Triangle C Rafting, would offer us an early-season discount, as much a tune-up for his own returning river rats and the new crew as anything else. Gillett was a good boss and had a solid reputation for running a tight and safe operation.

We'd divided the students up into rafts and attempted to balance the rafts equally with a combination of returning river rats, new crew, and students who had absolutely no experience at all in the wilderness. Mormon Bend was a perfect place to launch the rafts because there was plenty of time to smooth out any kinks with the guests before moving into the rapids. I'd worked summers as a river guide in southern Utah, and Ron asked if I wouldn't mind making a run with one of his new crew members that he was going to let guide his own raft in the upcoming summer months. "Just to kind of see how he does . . . how he is with guests," offered Ron. It was no problem at all.

No sooner had we launched than the weather started to turn. The students were well insulated with wet suits, life jackets, and layers of clothes. They'd stay warm because everybody contributed to paddling and had become, almost instantly, a member of the crew. We were the last raft, hanging back to pick up anybody who might go overboard during the run. Plowing through the rapids, the students could be heard screaming and flexing their newfound river muscle. There is something so wonderfully primal and empowering about being on the river, thinking that, to some degree, it can be tamed and you are part of this complex equation.

In a stretch of river called "Piece of Cake," our raft took a horrific gust of wind that virtually lifted the nose of the raft out of the water and put us at a dangerous angle for approaching a series of rapids. The guide barked out a series of quick commands, exactly the same as I would have done under the circumstance, but it was too late. In a split second, the raft flipped and we were all ejected into the icy water. I was sucked into a whirlpool and washing-machined over and over again. The force of the water ripped my tennis shoes from my feet and pulled my shorts down around my ankles. I was in deep trouble and I knew it.

Before ever getting on the river with clients, it is standard practice to acknowledge all the potential dangers and try to mitigate any accidents by offering safety and survival tips. While being sucked and swirled in the water, I could hear my own voice in a dull chorus of repetition so imbedded in me river trip after river trip these warnings had become merely sound bites. "If you get sucked into a whirlpool, don't fight the water. It is much stronger than you are. Relax and eventually the river will spit you out. Don't panic!" In the fray of it all, in the tumultuous bashing against rock and the disorientation that came with just such circumstance, it is almost impossible to practice. There is such a natural compulsion to fight the violence with struggle, it seems almost counterintuitive to relax. I wasn't able to practice my own advice and at the moment when I knew I could not hold my breath any longer, I actually laughed. I thought of my wife and children, the irony that this was one of the few raft trips where I was actually a guest and I was about to drown at my own game. In all the years on the water, I'd never flipped a raft and now, in this instant, I was about to drown. I exhaled and surrendered myself to the turbulence and was instantly spit up and out of the water, long enough to snatch a gasp of air before being pulled back down into the bosom of the Salmon.

The Captain's voice brought me back, "A couple of us are going to go out tomorrow and see if there is any place on the river we can spot fish. It isn't likely, but it's worth a try. I'll give you a call in the next day or so."

Two days later, the Captain called. The verdict hung in his voice and I knew how extremely difficult it was for him to admit the season had blown out. "I'm sorry, it's not going to happen this year."

"Damn," I cursed. "Son of a bitch!"

"I'm so sorry," he said, as though this had anything to do with him. The Captain is just such a man.

"I know it's selfish, but I'm just going to miss you and the boys."

"Me too."

There was something else on his mind. He cleared his throat before talking.

"You remember Jane's son, Mark?"

"Of course," I said, sort of annoyed he'd asked me. He knew that I knew them. Jane McCoy ran McCoy's fly-fishing and tackle shop in Stanley and I'd known Jane, her husband, and Mark for over twenty-five years. Mark was an accomplished musician who played for Mickey and the Motorcars and split his time between Stanley and Austin, Texas. He was also a terrific fly-fishing guide who had grown up on the river and knew it intimately. During steelhead season, he came back home to help his mother open up the shop and guide when he could.

"He drowned yesterday." I could hear the Captain choking back tears.

"What happened?" I was stupefied.

"He and a buddy wanted to go steelhead fishing but the river was too high and dangerous. They decided to take a raft and float the backside of Mormon Bend at night."

"So what happened, exactly?"

"They put in and began fishing. Coming around Mormon Bend they hit a submerged tree that slit the tubes and both men got thrown into the river. The one guy managed to swim to shore and they haven't found Mark's body."

"Jesus Christ! At Mormon Bend?" Then I asked, "How's Jane doing?"

"She's a wreck. A complete wreck." The Captain paused, trying to collect himself. "The whole town is broke up pretty bad."

"I'm so sorry. How do you ever survive something like this?"

"They're probably going to call off the search in a day or so and that will just kill Jane. She's been walking the river looking for Mark's body. You wouldn't even recognize her."

"That's so messed up."

"Worse than that. Mark's girlfriend is the head of Search and Rescue."

The Captain's kids had grown up with Mark so it gets personal pretty quickly in small towns. The other man and his dog that'd been thrown overboard managed to swim to safety. He'd worked for the Captain on his road crew for three and a half years.

When Search and Rescue called off the search, Mark's girlfriend and his mother continued on their own. A few days later, two steelhead fishermen found Mark's body in the back eddy below Sunbeam Dam.

Mark's girlfriend told a friend of ours that the best part of every day had been waking up in the morning and having Mark's head lying on her shoulder. And when she came upon his body in the Salmon River, it is exactly how she lifted him from the river.

What's Left?

I have survived. I'm not talking about surviving my own cancer, I'm talking about surviving this memoir. Cancer is easy, but writing an essay every single week for a full year is insane. I truly knew better when I started the collection but I've been feeling the press of time against me lately and it keeps me aware. Early morning has become a friend. Some of my most honest writing emerges in the unfolding light.

It's an interesting way to mark a year. Since the first essay what has surprised me most is how carefully I have paid attention to the everyday goings-on in the world around me. There are the cairns, the landmarks, those huge events that demand notation such as the birth of our first grandchild, Jack Fenton Kreitzer, and the subsequent birth of our second grandson, Finn Oliver Kreitzer, or the death of my father's brother Bill, my namesake whom I knew very little about. And the magic of birth and the mystery of death on both ends of these passages have been the great instructors.

The week our daughter was due to give birth to her first son, I was scheduled for major surgery related to my cancer. As both my oncologist and my surgeon warned, "This isn't a walk in the park by any means, Jeff. Things could go wrong in a hurry." It was a surgery I had to lobby vigorously for before it could be accepted as part of my standard of care. It wasn't in the protocol boundaries for the treatment of this disease and there were no guarantees that the surgery would change the trajectory of my cancer. But I had done my research and I believed I could make a compelling enough case for the surgery. It required that I argue my case in front of the hospital's Tumor Board. My personal physician and good friend, Dr. Andy Peiffer, did the lobbying for me. He was successful in building the case. Then I had to make an even more convincing argument with the insurance company that they should cover the expense. Once roadblocks were lifted, it was necessary to persuade a reluctant doctor who actually was one of the pioneers of this particular technique to perform the surgery.

The surgery wasn't a walk in the park. The surgeon nicked my vena cava and a forty-minute surgery became a two-hour surgery. This is, of course, an epic narrative of stubbornness in the face of medical protocols. Against the odds I was able to triumph over the system. I've become a pit bull in advocating for my own health issues and I trumpet the cause to challenge the system. But it takes a great deal of time and work to stay ahead of the game, to lobby the medical and insurance industries and fight with them. In this story, for a brief moment, I like to think I'm a hero. But I am not.

The hero of this story is my daughter, Bailey, and her husband, Dave, and most certainly, little Jack. When our daughter heard about my surgery and understood there could be some danger involved in the procedure, she pushed for an early delivery so I could hold our grandson in my arms and welcome him into this world before the operation.

To push the system as she did was not an easy proposition for a twenty-five-year-old woman. When she told the story to us, I knew the script by heart. I understood what she had to do and how, at every turn, the system would attempt to thwart her. As an educated patient she knew her rights. Jack was already full-term and it was imperative to her that I get to hold Jack in my arms; that maybe in the holding there would be a deep primitive connection calling me back from the brink. Holding Jack, red-faced and sing- ing only minutes after he was born, was such powerful medicine for me. She knew. Jack just celebrated his third birthday and I am still here.

My uncle Bill was the last sibling of my father's to die. By all measure, he should have been the first. During World War II he was severely wounded at Anzio Beach and was, for the most part, wheelchair-bound for the remainder of his life. He used the GI Bill to graduate from Harvard Law School and then practiced law in the dirt-poor, scrabble-hard town of Hobart, Oklahoma, where my father's family was raised.

Uncle Bill never left home and I could see this resentment in his early letters to my father. But there was never any self-pity and I do believe he lived a full and well-examined life.

My sister, herself a lawyer, was the executor for his estate. There wasn't much, really, but she did send me several boxes of correspondence between family members dating back to the early 1900s. My uncle never threw anything away. He was a packrat of epic hoarder proportion. Through him, through the letters my father and mother wrote to him, I am coming to understand my parents in a completely different light. My father and his family lived an impoverished life in Oklahoma. I can only remember visiting Hobart one time as a small child and it was enough. My paternal grandmother, Bertie Mae, was a tough, sinewy, shriveled, and unloving woman. She had a disfiguration of her right hand. Two fingers had been fused together during a barn fire when she was a small child, and she used this "claw" as punctuation when she talked to us. She frightened me. And against the persona of my maternal grandmother, Rosy, there was no comparison.

What is missing from my memoir is most interesting to me. Why did particular narratives appear on the page while others didn't? There is very little about my family living in Arabia during the early days of the Saudi awakening. I write this from my office where I'm sitting on a battered, hand-woven rug given to me by a Bedouin tribe and I've written zilch about it. Or, the base of a heavy copper booze still issued to my parents when we arrived in Dhahran that sits in the basement—and I write nothing. By the age of eleven, I had learned how to make sour mash and distill spirits, keeping the temperature constant at the stove and watching as distilled clear liquid dripped into glass jugs. How does that get left out of the collection in lieu of an essay, say, on the front door of my grandparent's subterranean apartment?

Then there was a three-month Bohemian trip in 1958 that my family took across Europe in a Volkswagen camper. Our plans were to include meeting my other Uncle Bill, my mother's brother, and his family in Italy. At the time, my uncle was stationed at Strategic Air Command forces in Wiesbaden, Germany. He was a "Top Gun" full of swagger and lived the fast life. Before getting married he reportedly had a serious fling with Italian actress Gina Lollobrigida. In anticipation of the rendezvous, my father sent what he thought was a humorous and benign Western Union telegram to my uncle's hotel. It read: "Troops will arrive fully prepared for serious hand to bottle combat. Stop. No prisoners will be left alive. Stop." The manager of the hotel became alarmed and turned over the telegram to the Polizia Municipale who arrested both of my parents because they believed it was an uprising of sorts. Money, American cigarettes, and booze set them free, not truth. Or seeing Hemingway at a bullfight in Madrid and not knowing or caring who he was, or my sister hanging upside down over the railing on the Eiffel Tower and she is an absolute klutz, or running a poker clinic when I lived in Oxford. What about the stolen bus, or running off with a carnival, or fly-fishing around land mines in Croatia with a young man who knew the river before it was poisoned by Milosevic's army, or getting drafted for Vietnam, or cutting off Riley's finger in the Forest Service, or . . . or . . . or? It doesn't stop once the floodgates are open.

I wrote from memory and circumstance. Many of the essays in this memoir surprised me and perhaps, of greater surprise, were how several spilled over on top of each other. Notably, I think of the Irish essays or my time in the Forest Service. Were these the most interesting of my narratives? I am not certain, but they surfaced and came to the paper so that tells me something.

Out of fifty-two essays, fifteen ended up on the cutting-room floor. Some they were too blemished or not sufficiently rendered for the collection. In place of these, I selected some essays I have a personal fondness for and I substituted these in good faith and humor. They have had lives in other publications and upon the revisiting have come back to life for me.

Much has been written on the subject and genre of creative nonfiction and I find myself asking the same question. Is this exactly the way it was? How can one ever answer such a question? It is loaded from the onset. Let me write this and I must credit my understanding to a good friend and fellow writer, Ron Carlson. Many years ago we sat together on a panel at a Writers@ Work conference in Park City, Utah. On this particular evening, the reading and post-reading discussion addressed the issue of humor in literature. Carlson read a hilarious short story called "Visigoths" and I read a humorous short story titled "Codpiece." One of the first questions following the reading was directed to Ron and it centered on the issue of "how much truth is there in your fiction?" Carlson thought for a moment and said, "Everything I write about is true, even the stuff I make up." The audience laughed, but I understood his response completely. We are the sum total of every dream, every imagination, and every truth and fiction in our life. When we tell our stories it is like starting over again, and in the end we can genuinely hope that we come close to truth.

Acknowledgments

I begin by thanking the Utah Arts Council for awarding me the 2010 first place award for personal essay and, most recently, the first place award for a full-length manuscript in creative nonfiction, originally titled *52 by 52, a memoir* and now, in its final iteration, *Requiem for the Living: A Memoir.* I thank the University of Utah Press for offering a publication prize along with this award and to editors John Alley and Glenda Cotter for their support.

As one might expect it to be, the task of writing fifty-two essays in fifty-two weeks is a daunting undertaking. And to imagine that all of them will be well-rendered enough, honed and polished enough to survive my own editorial concerns is a tall order. Some of the original essays are not yet ready to breathe on their own. They are still fragile and need further attention. In their place I have reworked some of my first essays regarding my own family. Iterations of these articles have appeared in other publications. I thank those editors who have always supported my work.

I am deeply indebted to Susen Sawatzki of Adnewsonline and Kelli Parker who first put their editorial eyes on my manuscript. Her comments were thoughtful and succinct. I would also like to thank those friends whose support helped me to continue in this madcap adventure. To my good friends and fellow writers David Kranes, Ron Carlson, Scott Carrier, and Maximilian Werner who have goaded and prodded me for several years to DO what I demand of writers and "stay in the room," I give humble thanks.

To Von and Virginia Whitby and Terry and Hans Carstensen, who unselfishly provided me with space to write in the most gorgeous of settings, a deep and humble tip of the hat.

A personal note of thanks to Brian Doyle, judge for the Utah Arts Council in the creative nonfiction category, who followed the thread in *52 by 52, a memoir* and offered thoughtful criticism and praise of this collection.

Finally, a hearty thanks to all those people who have entered my life and made me so much richer for the experience. Seriously, you know I'm talking about you.

Of course, without saying, my greatest appreciation and love to my own family. Thank you for staying the course with me.